PERFUME IN THE GARDEN

PERFUME IN THE GARDEN

by

Roy Genders

THE GARDEN BOOK CLUB
121 CHARING CROSS ROAD
LONDON W.C.2

TO
VICTOR AND CELIA

Printed in Great Britain by
The Camelot Press Ltd., London and Southampton

INTRODUCTION

THE many letters I have received on fragrance in the garden through articles which during the past months have appeared in various gardening journals and periodicals, has revealed the very great interest in this subject, and the fact that during the present century we have come to regard perfume in a plant as a very secondary consideration, the revival of interest is both surprising and pleasing. And so, when my publishers suggested that I should cover the subject in greater detail than could be the case in my articles, I jumped at the chance of writing a book that would perhaps be a help to those planning a new garden however small and to make a few suggestions that might one day bring mental comfort to the tired minds of those burdened by the troubles of the modern world. And for those who cannot see the beauty of flowers, but receive joy from their different scents, perhaps this little book offers a few helpful suggestions to those who construct our public gardens.

To the Editor of *The Queen, The Countryman, The Field, Country Fair,* and *Popular Gardening,* I offer my grateful thanks for permission to use certain material which has appeared in these journals during 1954.

I also thank Messrs. Allwood Brothers Limited for kindly allowing me to use the two delightful photos on pinks; and my typist, Doris Gatling, for her long hours sorting out the material from copious notes collected from my garden over a quarter of a century.

ROY GENDERS

CONTENTS

Chapter		Page
I.	Perfumes of the Garden	11
II.	A Garden of Fragrance	19
III.	Evening Perfume	24
IV.	Flowers of the Springtime	32
V.	Violets and Violas	42
VI.	Scented Annuals and Biennials	47
VII.	The Herbaceous Border	59
VIII.	Pinks and Other Fragrant Dianthus	69
IX.	Scented-Leaf Geraniums	82
X.	Perfume in Tulips	88
XI.	Bulbs with Perfume	93
XII.	The Herb Garden	102
XIII.	Scented Carpeting Plants	112
XIV.	Winter Fragrance	120
XV.	Aromatic Fruits	129
XVI.	The Butterfly Bush	137
XVII.	The Rose	141
XVIII.	Fragrant Trees	150
	Index	157

CHAPTER I

PERFUMES OF THE GARDEN

IT is said that the best things in this life are free and after paying my ten shillings for a seat to listen to the harsh voice of a platinum-haired woman singing through a raucous microphone to which accompaniment one is compelled to inhale the fumes from a thousand cigarettes, one is certain that the old adage has never been more true than today. Possibly the explanation of the cheerful manner of the countryman compared to that of his brother in the town is that he not only does not have to endure the foul smells of petrol and coal fires and thick green fogs, but he knows how to appreciate the sweet fragrance of the countryside. Compare the attitude of the West Countryman and those who live on the West Coast of Ireland with the unfortunate being who has to endure the ugliness and evil-smelling air of the Black Country. A period spent amidst the apple orchards of Somerset or Devon will find one's neighbour as mellow as a ripened Cox's Orange Pippin, smiling, courteous and helpful from sunrise to sunset. Time and money and the passing crowd have little meaning for him, there are more important things in life. The smell of heather as the wind blows from the Quantocks or across Dartmoor; the fragrance of bracken and moss of the woods along the banks of the Dart; the rich honey perfume of the flowers of the lime trees and of elder, of meadowsweet and new-mown hay; and of the apple orchards, especially in September with those half-rotten windfalls which give off such an aromatic perfume as they lie unheeded in the grass. From the cottage hearths come the fragrant smell of burning peat and apple wood. The perfume of the apple tree is wrapped up in our history. It was John Key, physician to Queen Mary, who wrote in 1552 imploring his fellow beings to "smell to an old sweet apple, for there is nothing more comforting to the spirits", and Ralph Austen, in his *Treatise of Fruit Trees* written exactly a hundred years later said "sweet perfumes work immediately upon the spirits for their refreshing, sweet and healthful ayres are special preservitives to health". Today we may write the same, for the difference in mental outlook between the West Countryman surrounded by his apple orchards and the Black Countryman surrounded by his slag heaps is not difficult for the stranger to determine.

After a period of work in London, it was recently my good fortune to arrive in Dublin after a twelve-hour journey by train and boat. The moment I stepped out of Westland Row Station I felt a feeling a relaxation difficult to understand until, after a meal, having set out for my eagerly awaited evening stroll along the banks of the Liffey, I realised why I had suddenly become so refreshed in spirit. Surely it was due to the fragrant smell of burning turf which even in some houses in Dublin is still burnt and whose smoke hangs over the city like incense. I saw little of note that evening— nothing, in fact, that I can remember except those barges used for bringing down the barrels of Guinness for export— but the perfume of the peat fires remains fresh to my senses to this day.

Likewise, the smell of burning apple wood in those clean, white-washed villages of Devon and Somerset; one is refreshed by it in the same way as one experiences a feeling of exhilaration from a walk over the moors of north Derbyshire and north Yorkshire where on any calm September day the aroma of the bracken and the bilberries and the musky fragrance of the purple heather is more refreshing than the most matured of wines. One would like to take a bottle of the fragrant air back to town to enjoy a little at the end of every stuffy day.

Perhaps our childhood days were happiest because we appreciated perfume more than we do in old age. The honey-suckle and the wild roses of the hedgerows; the pungent aroma of blackberries and mushrooms gathered on a September morn, still moist with dew; the primroses and violets for which we would search long hours after school, and if we obtained only one or two blooms we would smell them all the way home and be amply rewarded for our time. Now, in the evening of life, we like to sit back on a winter's evening and listen to the howling winds and the rains beating against the lead-light windows and we turn our thoughts back to schooldays, to the earthy smell of the freshly cut grass of the cricket field and the sweet fragrance of hay being cut in an adjoining field. The June weather then always seemed to be hot and the fragrance of the cut grass was most refreshing. Today we neither appreciate the value of perfume nor do we find time to enjoy these free luxuries though they are still there for the taking. Recently on a journey through Worcestershire, I stopped the car and got out to stretch my legs just before reaching the old Cathedral City of Worcester itself. At once the sweet perfume of a strawberry field in full fruit made me realise our strange conception of values in this present era. We pay half a sovereign to have our ear drums burst open and our lungs filled with stale tobacco smoke when all around us are perfumes to bring refreshment to a tired mind. Perhaps at the bottom of one's garden is a field of beans in full bloom or of clover, the white variety, for this possesses a much stronger honey-scent than the pink variety. Or not far away there might stand a plantation of pine trees, where their refreshing fragrance may be enjoyed to the full the whole year round. And in our gardens let there be sweet perfumed and aromatic plants for as Francis Bacon said "because the breath of flowers is far sweeter in the air (when it comes and goes, like the warbling of music) than in the hand, therefore nothing is more fit for that delight than to know what be the flowers and plants that do best perfume the air". And let there be plants which will provide the house with their fragrance throughout the winter too. If the garden be small, let it include some of the fragrant roses and some pinks for summer, bulbs with perfume and the quaint primroses for spring. Against a wall plant raspberry canes or a pear tree or two, and of course there must be a few rows of strawberries for the perfume of the fruit in summer and the aroma of the dying leaves in autumn. But don't neglect those plants which will give off their perfume when dried, lavender, southernwood, rosemary and thyme for their fragrance will be relished in the home during the days and nights of winter. The dried leaves of several of the mints mixed with those of bergamot and rosemary are excellent for bringing on sleep and bowls of lavender and dried rose petals placed in rooms about the house will keep one's mind fresh with their fragrance.

The larger garden may contain fragrant shrubs, the mock orange, the philadelphus, lilacs and sweet flowering winter shrubs. The shrub roses may be used and tall lilies. For the sweet perfume of their blossom in spring, apples should be planted, for again they are fragrant with their fruits in autumn. But whether one's garden is small or large, I would beg of you to make your selections from plants which possess perfume as well as colour. There is a wide range from which to choose, and yet the question of perfume in the garden is so rarely thought about. It is worth spending a little time when selecting one's roses for after all they do remain in your garden for almost a lifetime, to select those with an attractive scent in addition to their habit and colour. One of the best all round roses in my garden during the very difficult summer of 1954 was Tahiti, a new rose which bears a huge amber-yellow bloom, shaded with pink on the outside edges of the petals. It stood up to periods of drought and heavy rains giving off its sumptuous rich lily-like perfume. And yet it is a rose that has not yet won universal fame, why I do not know, for its foliage is rich and glossy and is not troubled with mildew even in the wettest of weather. But today it is rarely that consideration is given to perfume, if a plant just happens to have it when it has been planted then so much the better, or it may not even then be noticed as being fragrant. The peony is another example of a plant, several varieties of which possess rich fragrance, whilst others have none. Those with perfume being equally as lovely as those without it, it is difficult to see why they are not preferred, but our appreciation of scent seems to have vanished and not only our gardens are the poorer but we ourselves, for it is little use our bodies being refreshed if not our minds. The gardeners of the first Elizabethan era realised this but not those of the second Elizabeth. Even as far back as 2500 B.C. and right up to the Birth of Christ, the Egyptians placed fragrant leaves and flowers in the tombs of their kings and queens which in many cases preserved their fragrance until discovered in our own days. But of course, these people valued their incense trade above all other trades which was coveted by the rest of the then known world. We read in the Bible of spikenard, incense, cinnamon and myrrh, spices which were valued above all things. Later our own monasteries held the herbs we know today in reverence and with the Norman Invasion came methods of distillation. Thus only flowers with perfume were grown, the violet, the rose, lilies and wallflowers and these flowers remained favourites together with the herbs, in our cottage gardens down to late Victorian days when the scented-leaf geranium was so popular for making up bags of fragrant leaves and flowers. Soon the harsh scarlet blooms of Paul Crampel were to remove the more modest scented geranium from popularity and whilst our homes lost much of their charm we gradually lost the art of appreciating not only fragrant smells but flavour in our food. Succulent meats flavoured with an assortment of aromatic herbs have been replaced by boiled mutton, cabbage boiled in water and mashed potatoes, and we revel in it. Likewise those strongly spiced apples, Devonshire Quarrenden, D'Arcy Spice and Cornish Aromatic, have been replaced by imported fruit with shining skins which cheat the housewife into believing that they will make delicious eating when in fact they are almost completely devoid of flavour. In any case, it is possibly cheaper to buy one's fruit and there is far less labour connected with a packet of shop herbs than with growing and drying one's own, however superior the quality might be, so why worry. But a community devoid of sweet and aromatic smells is like a ship without a rudder, it may drift along but something is sadly missing. Parkinson thought the same and in his *Paradisus* he writes: "That as many herbs and flowers with their fragrant sweet smells do comfort and as it were revive the spirits and perfume a whole house. . . ." Right through mediaeval times when herbs and flowers were used to cover the musty, dank floors of places of worship and dwelling, mention was made by writers of the freshening of "the spirits" as equal in importance to the sweetening of the house. And whilst we may not need the fragrant plants today for sweetening our homes, we still do need them for reviving our spirits.

Eleanour Sinclair Rohde has said that "fragrance in flowers

may be described as their music". I feel that it is their way of expressing their individual characteristics, that it is their way of talking to us and I am sure a blind person will feel the same way when walking through a fragrant garden. The scent of every flower or fragrant-leaved plant is a reminder of past joys. The buddleia, so loved by butterflies, thrives along our coasts as nowhere else. There it scents the air with its pleasant musty fragrance and wherever I enjoy its August perfume it is always a reminder of seaside holidays. Even if in the midst of the industrial Midlands the scent of the buddleia brings back memories of a foamy sea and silver sands, of days when you could get a massive ice cream for a penny and spend half an hour licking it.

Recently I received through the post a few sprigs of lad's-love (southernwood) for identification and immediately it was as if the years had stopped a quarter of a century ago and I was back in my grandparents' garden in Derbyshire, where lad's-love grew in large dense bushes. The cottage and its typical garden were high above the rest of the village, like those charming white-washed cottages clustered round the church at Minehead in Somerset and in the half-light of evening the fragrance from the chimney smoke as it reached the cottage in long spirals of grey mist combined with the perfume of the herbs, of the evening primroses and of stocks, sweet-williams and pinks, it was almost overpoweringly delicious. Happy days indeed, when one could enjoy the fragrance until darkness fell rocking to and fro on the old swing, chewing at sprigs of peppermint and sage, or pressing the scented leaves of geraniums, rosemary and lad's-love. And I feel that blind people, and indeed those who possess their sight, re-live past days, possibly happier days, when they come into contact with a scented plant, memories being more fragrant even than the scent of the plants. Perhaps in years ahead we may decide that pleasant perfumes are as important to the human race as pleasant things to eat, those of ancient days thought them more so, and then our public parks and gardens will be planted with fragrant plants for all and particularly the blind to enjoy. A plant with perfume is no more expensive than one which is entirely devoid of scent, is no more difficult to grow and gives us additional pleasures to revive and freshen our minds and bodies, and yet each year we put less value on things with a pleasant scent. Perhaps we have lost our sense of smell as well as our appreciation of pleasing perfumes.

There is another note on which to end this chapter, something that in these days we tend to neglect and that is the fun to be obtained from a walk down the garden when work is done for the day, our own fun made in exactly the same way as when we were children. Recently I was staying with an old countryman in his tiny oak-beamed cottage, the rooms darkened by the scented-leaf geraniums which were in every window, and each evening on his return from his work in the fields he would take a full pint of cider and in silence and with a smack of the lips would say, whatever the weather: "Well, are you ready?" That was the signal for which I had been waiting all day, for a walk in his old world garden before dusk. In spring we would enjoy a more delicate perfume, the sweet smell of broad beans in flower, of violets and primroses hiding amongst the new growth of the herbaceous plants for the garden was typical of the old world cottage, entirely without any order which made it all the more exciting. There would be daffodils in plenty and apple blossom, a few wallflowers growing as perennials and the leaves of rosemary, lavender and bay, in fact, all the plants known to Elizabethan gardens. The poet Spencer delightfully draws a picture of these sweetly perfumed plants and incidently refers to the old double green primrose:

> "Upon her head a cremosin coronet
> With Damask roses and Daffodillies, set,
> Bay leaves between,
> And primroses greene,
> Embellish the sweet violet."

In late July, the perfumes would be stronger. There was the rich scent of the deep crimson roses and the powerful fragrance of the Madonna lilies and of stocks. If the air was still it was almost overwhelming. Then in autumn, the fragrance was more aromatic, more pungent, with the ripened herbs, the autumn fruiting raspberries and the dying strawberry leaves. The honeysuckle, "whose scent represents the soul of the dew" and the late sown mignonette, which in the words of Maurice Maeterlinck "that silently distils perfumes that give us a foretaste of the air we breathe on the threshold of Paradise". So do they all combine in perfect harmony to give us this reminder. And what fun those walks down his old garden were, seeking out flowers half hidden by a neighbouring plant, squeezing the leaves of others to make them give of their aromatic scent, popping into one's mouth a strawberry, or a fully ripened gooseberry, not the flavourless fruits of today, but those packed with fragrance, sweet and juicy like Black Prince strawberry and Red Champagne gooseberry. In late autumn my friend would say: "Try that", pointing to a matured russet apple, possibly D'Arcy Spice, which looked so unattractive and misshapen, but its aroma and crispness upon eating made our handsome looking, imported apples eat like cotton wool. We would spend about an hour and then come in for tea or supper, depending upon the time of the year. "That's done me good", my friend would always say, whilst he lit the lamp or untied his boots and I would sit down in a rocking chair at the other side of the log fire and before long I should be fast asleep. This old countryman lived to be a ripe age and enjoyed every moment of his simple pleasures, his glass of cider and his fragrant garden, and upon every visit he would remind me that "The best things in life are free, lad", and how true it is.

CHAPTER II

A GARDEN OF FRAGRANCE

A T the end of my garden divided from the usual lawns, rose beds and herbaceous borders by a 6-ft. wall and a row of silver birches, is an almost square piece of ground about 50 ft. long. For several years I left it as I found it, overgrown with nettles and couch. Then it came to me one summer evening when the smell of wild honeysuckle filled the air; why not make of this waste plot a garden of fragrance? Through the autumn and winter, while the work of clearing it went on, I made copious notes, so that I had a scheme well in mind before I ordered the plants.

There would be two borders, one herbaceous and the other a shrubbery backed by trees, with a bed of herbs connecting the two at the lower end. A raised bed of Ena Harkness roses would form the centre-piece, set in a lawn surrounded by crazy paving. The plants would have to be perennial, needing as little labour as possible. The garden being small, I would avoid any with a tendency to rampant growth; and, as the site was exposed I would have to reject all things tender; several of the highly perfumed magnolias, for example, and those viburnums which are not truly hardy.

For a winter-flowering shrub my first choice was *Viburnum fragrans*, which grows about 6 ft. high, needs little pruning and carries from November to February white tubular blooms sweetly scented. It would be followed by the little-known *Viburnum carlesii*, from Korea. This seldom grows taller than 4 ft. and is not too happy in a soil with lime; nor does it like cold winds. But in the shelter of a hurdle, fence or hedge it bears in early spring a profusion of flowers with carnation scent, especially noticeable after a shower of rain. In late autumn its foliage turns a brilliant scarlet. It is therefore, well worth a trial, even though it may not succeed. Another lovely shrub is the evergreen Japanese *viburnum* (*V. henryi*), whose lemon-scented flowers in midsummer are followed by bright red berries.

For winter fragrance I chose also witch-hazel, of which there are several charming species. Possibly the most valuable is *Hamamelis Virginiana,* which grows to a height of from 10-12 ft. producing its pale yellow sweetly scented flowers in October and November, when there is little perfume in the garden. Most of us know the species *mollis,* but *vernalis,* is more graceful in habit and its foliage turns an attractive bright yellow in autumn. Small crimson flowers tinged with yellow appear from Christmas until March and carry a powerful perfume, especially enjoyable if a sprig is taken indoors.

Early spring fragrance was to be provided by daphnes. We all know the richly coloured *D. mezereum,* though we may despair of its ever reaching a worth-while size. It was suggested to me that I should plant instead the variety Somerset, in all soils a stronger grower, which bears clusters of bright rosy-pink flowers in May. Its perfume is even stronger than that of *mezereum.*

A little-known but extremely hardy plant that deserves wider recognition is the evergreen *Osmarea Burkwoodii;* its box-like foliage is crowded with fragrant white blooms during May, a sparse month in the garden. It does well in any soil and is particularly suitable for a small hedge. In a lime-free soil a most handsome shrub, excellent in a shady corner, is *Pieris Forrestii,* which is not only evergreen, with blossom of delicious fragrance, but has the distinction of vivid crimson leaves in summer.

For summer fragrance I decided to include mock orange (*Philadelphus*). Several varieties possess an unpleasantly powerful scent, but the rich Jersey-cream coloured flowers of *P. coronarius,* have a delicate orange perfume. *Belle Etoile* produces on long arching sprays rather like those of a buddleia, white, flushed purple blooms, with a fragrance resembling a pineapple's. I would also plant buddleias for their perfume and graceful habit, as abundantly as space permitted.

The lilac hybrids need almost no attention after planting; more lilacs are spoilt by overpruning than any other shrub. They like a soil richer in humus than most and should be left to grow as they will, with ample room for development. As space was limited, I chose five of different colours. First came the new variety Primrose, which bears a profusion of rich yellow blooms that seem to carry a true primrose fragrance; but it has made little progress as yet and may be too slow-growing. An old favourite, Charles Joly, with long fully double spikes, is still the best of the rich purples, and the strongly perfumed Madame Lemoine, the best of the double whites. I also included the double silver-pink Lucie Baltet, the first lilac to flower and the new pale blue Clarke's Giant, which has the largest flower spikes of any lilac. This completed the shrubbery, lavenders being reserved for the herbaceous border, but to cover a stone arch I planted a wintersweet (*Chimonanthus fragrans*), to flower from Christmas to March. This may be grown as a small shrub, though it makes quicker growth on a sheltering wall.

As edging for the shrubbery I chose catmint and for the herbaceous border old-fashioned pinks. Both are best planted in early April when they will begin to grow away at once, making large bushy plants by the end of summer. One of the loveliest and most fragrant of the old pinks is Glory of Lyonaise, whose double shell-pink blooms have attractive deep cream centres. Jane Austen, is a single of rich mulberry colour, fringed white. The old Victorian may be likened to a cabbage rose, for it bears a huge cabbage-like white bloom, heavily laced jet black, with tremendous perfume. For contrast the glowing double Red Emperor, maroon with crimson eye, is a beauty.

I made lilies the basis of the herbaceous border, planting them in clusters of three with the taller varieties at the back. In April, when I had worked plenty of leaf mould into the deeply dug soil, I planted the bulbs 8 inches apart and 6 inches deep on sand, filling in with peat. I bought only varieties noted for hardiness, easy-doers and quite inexpensive. Toward the back of the border I planted *Lilium regale*, and its pure white counterpart; Maxwill for its brilliant orange flowers in late July; the Californian lily, *L. pardalinum giganteum*, with its blooms of vivid scarlet and purple markings at the centre; and *L. henryi*, for August flowering. Several are only slightly fragrant, but all are superb border plants. In front are *L. cernuum*, noted for its dainty lilac-pink blooms; two varieties of *L. pumilum*, the scarlet one known to our gardens about a hundred years ago and Golden Gleam; and as a contrast *L. speciosum album*, a particular favourite of mine with flowers of purest white, striped green, and attractive chocolate coloured anthers. Lilies bloom year after year, the only attention required being some staking in early summer and a peat mulch after flowering in autumn.

Lavenders were planted in the border during March, the best time for moving them in an exposed garden. I managed to find a dozen, ranging from the dwarf blue, pink and mauve Hidcote varieties, which take a long time to reach a height of 1 ft. to the tall Grappenhall, ideal for a hedge and worth growing for its blooms; it is the darkest of all lavenders. Useful as a contrast and almost as vigorous is the pure white variety, *alba*.

One of the most pleasantly perfumed of all plants is the Chilean *Verbena corymbosa*, which seems quite hardy in Britain if a few fronds of bracken are placed over the roots during severe weather. These spread with great freedom and it quickly forms a large bushy plant which is covered in late summer with a mass of flowers carrying the true verbena scent. Bergamots, too, are deliciously aromatic and require just an ordinary soil and no staking. Two new varieties, the clear rose, Croftway Pink, and the dark crimson, Mahogany, keep excellent company with the more common but equally lovely Cambridge Scarlet. I planted with them in groups the violet-blue garden sage, *Salvia nemorosa*. A rare plant, easily grown, is *Delphinium brunonianum*, a native of the Himalayas. It produces on 2-ft. stems, flowers of palest sky-blue, and its strangely hairy foliage has a rich musk aroma that is especially pronounced after a July shower. With it I have planted the sweetly perfumed peony, *Duchesse de Nemours*, its large double creamy-white flowers being, in mid-summer, as lovely as their perfume. About the border are masses of *Iris Reticulata*, which produces scented violet-and-orange flowers in late winter.

The small herb garden was included because of its value

in the kitchen, as well as its fragrance outdoors and in. Rosemary and hyssop; sage and lemon thyme; the camphor plant and eau-de-Cologne mint, with camomile in the gaps between the crazy paving, for the more it is trodden, the more it exhales its fragrance. A herb garden is, of course, a story to itself.

CHAPTER III

EVENING PERFUME

THERE is no more wholesome scent than that of the stack-yard, which adjoins my garden and never is the fragrance of matured hay more pleasant than during early summer. By then there is only a small portion of a stack left and there it will remain exposed to winds and rain until the cattle are indoors again in October when it will be used before the new season's stacks. It would be disappointing if there was none of the old hay left over each summer, for the summer rains and gentle breezes would fall only on the untidy ground and there would be no sweet fragrance of the hay to drift across the garden. But there would still be the pine trees which surround that side of the garden overlooking the sea, protecting the plants from the salty sea breezes and diffusing their delicate pine fragrance over the whole garden. These scents are always present, their perfume being wholesome and invigorating, but there are others which combine to make the evening garden in early summer even more delightful. In the border the bergamot, and evening primroses are especially delightful when the sun has cast its longest shadow over the lawn and has almost disappeared. The evening primroses then come into the fullness of flower which they deny us during hours of full daylight. Their pale yellow colouring is almost moon-like, their rich perfume overpowering in a sheltered garden on a calm evening. They still shine bright as the moon casts its cold rays across the sea and remain so until the night gives way to the day once more. Then they close up and completely lose their beauty.

Plant with them the night-scented stock, *Matthiola bicornis*, a hardy annual, which should be sown as an edging to, or in clumps, about the border. Sow early in April then from mid-June onwards through the summer the fragrance of their mauve and white flowers will fill the garden. It is surprising what perfume their tiny flowers give off. Wherever possible I sow the seed near a window, as an edging to a bed of Intermediate stocks, so that the full perfume of these stocks can enter the rooms in the early evening. After rain or when the hose-pipe may have been used at sundown, their fragrance is terrific. Those who live in a bungalow, or who may sleep downstairs, should always fill the flower beds outside the window with all forms of stocks and against the wall plant the biennial evening primrose, then inhale their perfume throughout the night and in the morning awake refreshed in body and in spirit.

One of the richest scented of all evening perfume flowers is the half-hardy annual *Nicotiana affini*, the tobacco plant, though not the plant which provides us with tobacco which is *Nicotiana virginiana*. *N. affini*, is a tall growing annual often attaining a height of 4 ft. and it bears unattractive white star-shaped blooms which, like the evening primrose, open only at nightfall. But though the blooms are insignificant, their fragrance is amazingly rich and spicy, especially when grown in a rich soil. The plants should be given the usual half-hardy treatment and should be planted out late in May, towards the back of a border spacing them 10 inches apart. The leaves, though large and of the familiar tobacco-leaf shape are handsome in the border, acting as a background to more colourful plants so that they have their use during the daytime as well as at night.

Of quite recent introduction is a variety called Daylight, the blooms remaining fully open during daytime, and though not quite so strongly perfumed as the original, the larger pure white blooms are more attractive. A dwarf white bedding variety, a miniature counterpart of Daylight, and deliciously scented has been evolved and should become a most popular bedding plant for it flowers on stems less than 12 inches tall and what is more, it keeps on flowering right into autumn being fragrant both by day and by night.

Another species of the tobacco plant, *Nicotiana sylvestris*, makes a most handsome plant, often reaching a height of more than 6 ft. and is better left to a large garden. It bears very large leaves and large creamy-white flowers which are extremely fragrant at nightfall.

It is said that today few seed catalogues list that charming old perennial, the sweet rocket, *Hesperis matronalis*, so frequently found in old cottage gardens, but now almost extinct. William Robinson, the famous gardener, thought it "amongst the most desirable of garden flowers". The sweet rocket, is a hardy perennial but unlike most, in that it is necessary to move it each year; it is a perennial with the habit of an annual and is easily grown from seed sown outdoors late in April, also cuttings may be taken and they root quite easily in a sandy soil. The plant is valuable in that it grows well in partial shade and may be planted freely in the shrub border, provided the soil contains plenty of humus, for like most shade preferring plants, the sweet rocket, enjoys a moist soil. The plants grow to a height of 3 ft. and bear either white or purple flowers, which seem to give of their violet-like perfume only at nightfall, or if in almost full shade. Due to its rich violet fragrance, it was known as Dame's violets, by our grandparents, another of those delightful names which really have more meaning than those we give to our plants today.

I am always baffled by the ability of certain flowers to fill the air with their fragrance at nightfall, yet during daytime we do not notice their fragrance though several of these plants do open their blooms in the sunlight. One is the night-scented campion, *Lychnis vespertina*, which like all the campions is a lover of a chalky soil and may be found growing wild in various parts of Britain. In the evening it exhales its heavy fragrance for which it is worth a place in the garden if not for its rather uninteresting flowers. A perennial similarly found in the wild state in Scotland, is *Linnarea borealis*, the Twin Flower, so called because each stem bears two little drooping flowers, creamy-white, flushed pink and which smell strongly of meadowsweet in the evening. With its trailing evergreen habit, this is a delightful plant for planting between crazy paving stones, or used as an edging to a shrubbery but it is only happy in a dry, acid soil, such as is so often found in town gardens. There its grows rampant, for it enjoys similar conditions to that of the Scottish pine woods where it is to be found growing wild if in rather a different atmosphere!

The sand verbenas, the abronias, are not common plants.

They have a trailing habit and are natives of California. They are delightful when used for trailing down a dry wall, especially *Abronia latifolia*, which bears heads of pale yellow flowers which in the evening smell powerfully of honey and remain in bloom from mid-July until well into autumn. Another species *A. fragrans*, is not of trailing habit as are most of the other species, but grows to a height of almost 2 ft. bearing white flowers which open only at sundown, breathing out a pleasant vanilla perfume. These two abronias, like a humus-laden loam, and in a warm area may be treated as perennials, which they are really, though in Northern gardens they should be given half-hardy annual treatment, for they grow readily from seed and will be in bloom by August 1st.

Those who have a stream running through the garden or are blessed with a pond, or a moist, shady border, will find that several of the Asiatic primulas give out a delightful delicate fragrance by night as well as by day. They are charming plants of easy culture and for a moist position they are without a peer. Several carry no distinct perfume, others do, and none is sweeter than *P. Sikkimensis*, which was discovered growing in the Himalyas at a height of nearly 20,000 ft. The beautiful primrose-yellow blooms are borne on 2 ft. stems from tufts of long, narrow, dark green leaves. To see them at their best and to drink the sweetness of their perfume to the full, the plants should be massed. This will present no difficulties, for the plants readily increase by self-sown seed and may also be increased by division after flowering. Flowering from late June until late in August, this must be the last of the primulas to bloom. Though lovely during the daytime, the pale yellow umbels look superb in the fading light of a July day when their perfume takes on an added richness. This is a plant that can be planted in almost the full shade of trees, but if this is done, the plants must never be allowed to suffer from dry conditions which so often happens, for not only do trees in full leaf shield off the strong sunlight, but also gentle summer rains. I always feel that *P. Sikkimensis*, is happiest with its feet in moisture and its head in no more than dappled shade. A humus-laden soil is most important and if this does not naturally contain plenty of leaf mould, then mix in some well rotted manure and some peat or plenty of decayed leaves, anything in fact that will retain moisture throughout summer.

A native of Tibet and requiring conditions similar to *P. Sikkimensis*, is *P. florindae*, which bears its sulphur-yellow hanging bells on 3-ft. stems, and especially during evening are they sweetly fragrant. In all ways it may be said to be a large *Sikkimensis*, for its flower heads are bigger so are its leaves, whilst its perfume, especially after rain is richer and may be enjoyed at a distance. The plants like partial shade and as wet a soil as it is possible to get without it being stagnant. Working into the soil plenty of peat or leaf mould is the secret of success with these moisture loving primulas. *P. Florindae*, blooms during early summer and so will ensure the continuation of the flowering season of these charming plants throughout summer.

Another moisture loving primula is *P. helodoxa*, called by the Chinese, The Glory of the Marsh. Its rich yellow blooms are borne on tiers on 2-ft. stems and like the others it sows its own seed in quantity. It is not so richly fragrant though to come upon a bed of the plant growing by the waterside in the evening twilight is a sight of great beauty.

A sweetly scented primula which requires completely different treatment is *P. nutans*, which likes a soil containing some humus though when dormant the plant will rot away if the plant is not given complete drainage. It should, therefore, be given a raised bed facing north and the plant is so deliciously scented that it is well worth covering during mid-winter with a garden light which will keep off excessive moisture. The plant bears large lavender bells covered, like the leaves, in meal, and what an enchanting perfume they give off during late afternoon.

Another lovely primula which is remarkably sweet scented at night, is the old double primrose, Marie Crousse, described in the chapter on spring perfumes. At night it is especially delicious and I well remember the fragrance of a small bed in the courtyard of an old manor house, reminding me as I arrived at dusk of the honeysuckle, yet another plant whose flowers carry a richer fragrance at eventide than during the day. No plant covers a stone gateway quite like the honeysuckle, blending with the stonework as only the rose and the honeysuckle can do, the "twisted eglantine" of Milton's *L'allegro*. So many of those grassy banks found somewhere in most large gardens could be covered with the trailing and rapidly growing honeysuckle and the fragrance of the flowers enjoyed through springtime and early summer. The vigorous, free flowering species, *Lonicera Caprifolium*, is the best for covering a bank and it will be just as profuse with its blooms when growing in a sunless northerly position as when in full sun but will it be so fragrant? Shakespeare in *Much Ado About Nothing* tells us of ". . . Honeysuckles, ripened by the sun" in which he suggested the need for sunshine to bring out the maximum fragrance in the flowers. The flowers of *L. Caprifolium* are large, creamy-yellow and beautifully scented, turning to vivid orange berries in early autumn.

A particularly lovely variety is the free flowering *Lonicera grata*, the blooms being cream flushed with pink. It is the last of all the honeysuckles to bloom and is valuable in extending the season. But perhaps the most fragrant of all are the early Dutch *L. belgica* and the later flowering Dutch, *L. serotina*, both of which bear large whorled clusters of heavily fragrant creamy-yellow flowers which open from attractive crimson buds. The early Dutch commences to bloom in early May and continues throughout summer, the late Dutch once called the Flemish honeysuckle, first blooms mid-June and will still be giving of its rich evening fragrance well into autumn. For mid-summer perfume, the common honeysuckle, *L. periclymenum*, of which the Dutch are different forms, may be enjoyed and also the species with the attractive mottled foliage, *L. japonica aureo reticulata*, whose name reads more like a book of Virgil than that of a simple garden plant. The leaves are mottled with gold and its rich yellow flowers are strongly scented, though of quite different form from the other species of honeysuckle. The shape of the leaves too, is different, resembling the oak-leaved honeysuckle which is a variety of the common form. Yet another characteristic is that it is evergreen which gives the Japanese honeysuckles an additional value in covering an unsightly trellis. The species *L. Halleana*, which produces long twining branches and bears pure white flowers on the tips of the young shoots may also be used for covering a trellis. It is evergreen but being a native of Eastern China, it does not appear to be quite as hardy as the others and should be confined to sheltered gardens. But do plant as many of these scented honeysuckles as your garden will accommodate, let them entwine the trellis or hurdles which may surround the herb garden or may be used for sheltering the border. Or train them up the walls of a house, preferably on trellis and so let their evening fragrance drift through the open windows.

Another lovely fragrant climbing plant is the jasmine. For mid-winter flowering, when they bear their clear golden-yellow blooms on long leafless sprays, there must be few gardens where *Jasmine nudiflorum* does not grow. During the darkest January days even before the individual blooms are open, the sprays may be taken indoors to open in water and provide fragrance in the bedroom. But in how many gardens is to be found the sweetly honey-scented summer flowering species, *J. officinale major*, which is evergreen and which bears clusters of pure white blooms from late in June until into autumn and how richly fragrant they are at night. No plant is lovelier than this with the harvest moon shining on its clusters of paper white flowers, with the air almost still and when the sweet smell of the blossom will be carried for a considerable distance. This is a rapidly growing plant and should be used more frequently to cover the bare brick walls of the many new houses. Another vigorous species which blooms during late summer is *J. stephanense*, which covers itself with small pink flowers which are only slightly scented.

For the small garden, where their rich perfume can be enjoyed to the full, the old fashioned heliotrope is a charming plant and of easy culture. But it should be grown in a small walled garden, even a town garden where the winds will not diffuse its fragrance. Before this sophisticated age, it used to be called cherry pie and there was as wide a range of varieties as for geraniums. But the plant fell from favour on account of its rather unsignificant violet-blue flowers, just as some of those small deliciously aromatic and sweet gooseberries have been replaced by those large coarse fruiting varieties possessing little or no flavour. But what a treat we miss, for there is no perfume like that of the heliotrope nor are they of difficult culture. They may be treated like half-hardy annuals and sown in gentle heat early in March, pricked off and planted outside towards the end of May or better still lift a few plants late in September, winter them in pots containing a sandy soil in a frost proof room or greenhouse, then bring them into new growth early in spring when the new shoots may be struck in a compost containing a mixture of peat and sand. They will quickly root and should be potted into individual pots during April. Mid-May they should be removed to a cold frame for hardening as should all half-hardy plants and they will be ready for the open ground at the month end. They thrive in a dry, loamy soil and like best a position of semi-shade. They bloom profusely throughout late summer and are beloved by bees and butterflies, but it is in the evening, with the late summer dew on them that the blossoms are most fragrant, like stocks a bed will perfume the air for a distance. Two charming varieties for planting together are the deep violet, Valencia, and the pure white, White Lady. The heliotrope is certainly one of those flowers "sweeter in the air than in the hand . . . where it comes and goes like the warbling of music" in the words of Francis Bacon and I think the same may be said of all those flowers which are particularly fragrant at night. At the end of a tiring day their perfume "is the greatest refreshment to the spirits of man", yet, do we prefer the foetid atmosphere of the cinema.

CHAPTER IV

FLOWERS OF THE SPRINGTIME

AFTER the long winter days, the first flowers of springtime are awaited. I do not mean the bulbs which have of course as much to do with springtime fragrance as the other flowers of woodland and meadow. Here I am thinking of the primrose and the violet and the auricula, whose delicate perfume reminds one of the woodland glades where they are happiest. A bunch of primroses gathered whilst the showers of April are still falling, smells of moss, bracken and dead leaves more than it does of any particular flower. Only a few primrose varieties possess a distinct perfume, but all may be said to carry the distinct fragrance of the woodlands. It is an invigorating perfume, reminding one of busy days ahead in the garden and of cold spring winds, quite different from the musky, lazy perfume of woodland and garden in autumn, when every falling leaf can be heard in the calm stillness of the afternoon. We think then of log fires, oat-cakes and books. But spring is an exciting time, for in all parts of the garden, beneath the still almost leafless trees, behind stones and amidst short grass are to be found primroses and violets of every colour. These are the plants children love best, they are small and neat, yet colourful and fragrant. These same plants too have been known to English children since mediaeval times when they were cultivated for their medicinal and cleansing properties. Parkinson tells us that "the juice of the flowers [primroses] is commended to cleanse spots of the face, whereof some gentlewomen have found good experience". And what delightful names they were given—hose-in-hose, Jack-in-the-Green, which have been handed down to this day. Ideal plants for window-boxes, trough gardens, for an edging to a path, for planting about the rockery, there is no wonder that there has been a tremendous revival of the primrose, since the ending of the war, for it is a plant native to our country and particularly suited to the damp climate.

Though it is said that some of them are difficult to grow, the reason for their being almost unknown to gardeners of the first half of the twentieth century seems to be twofold; the scarcity of humus in our gardens, and their slow propagating qualities compared with plants such as michaelmas daisies and polyanthus in an age when most nurserymen conduct their business by mail order, and "quick returns" are the order of the day. But that a number of these lovely primroses have been allowed to become almost extinct, as indeed several varieties appear to be completely so, is nothing short of tragic. No Tudor knot garden was without its double primroses, which evidence we have from one of the earliest of all writers on gardening subjects, Tabernaemontanus, who was familiar with the double sulphur primrose in the year 1500. The great Elizabethan gardener John Gerard, illustrated the double white, *alba plena*, in his *Historie of Plants*, published in 1597, that same variety still to be found in English gardens today. Parkinson in his *Paradisi in Sole* (1629) describes this same primrose as "like unto the field primrose, but very thicke and double, and of the same sweet scent with them". Thirty years later, John Rea in his *Flora*, writes of the double primrose, "were it not so common in every country-woman's garden, it would be more respected, for indeed it is a sweet and dainty double flower and the chiefest of all our English kinds".

Right up to the beginning of the twentieth century these lovely flowers flourished in gardens of cottage and manor in all parts of Britain, for they will grow in any soil provided they receive some humus. They enjoy best a soil deeply cultivated to which has been incorporated some nitrogenous manure, which will not only feed the plants, but will also retain much needed moisture in the soil during dry weather. An excellent compost is one of peat, thoroughly mixed with dry poultry manure and decayed leaves, a mixture which should not be difficult to obtain. Old mushroom bed compost and of course well rotted farmyard manure is ideal, but where this is difficult to obtain, and one gardens within easy reach of the sea, then seaweed will prove of value and for the country-man chopped pea and bean haulm mixed with some peat will

c

supply the necessary nitrogen. The townsman may use spent hops with equally good results. But what is more important is to use these ingredients also as a top dressing or mulch during early summer of each year and failure to do so is why the double primroses have, during the past fifty years, earned the reputation of being "difficult". For they form their new season's roots almost at the point where the soil is level with the crown, the old rootstock being gradually discarded and playing no part in nourishing the plant. If a mulch is not given each year or at the most every alternate year, these tiny new roots will not only be devoid of nourishment, but may perhaps be killed by a hot summer sun. It follows that the plant will also die back due to lack of food and water for the original rootstock will soon play no part in the life of the plant. In the old cottage gardens, manure and humus in some form would be thrown over the plants on many occasions for there was more available manure than the land had need of. As our population increased and it was a question of growing more and more food, there was little available for flowering plants and the double primrose died out in consequence and few gardeners realised why. A new generation of gardeners grew up who had no knowledge at all of the double primrose, but the experiments of one or two enthusiasts who for some considerable time had treasured their collections, brought about an enthusiastic revival for here was a plant that if given some humus, was ideal for the small garden, for besides being suitable as an edging to paths and small flower beds, and for window-box display, or planted in a cold corner facing north or east, or round stems of apple trees where they enjoy conditions of semi-shade during the heat of summer, they will increase rapidly, one two year-old root producing up to a hundred blooms during spring and early summer. At almost any time of the year they may be planted, but to have them at their brilliant best during springtime, the early autumn does seem to be the most suitable time. The old rootstock should be removed but not discarded, for if planted like the rhizome of an iris with the severed end at soil level, they will frequently sprout in early spring and form fresh roots at soil level. Firm, but not too deep planting will be appreciated by the plants.

The roots may be divided every third year, or every year if one wishes to increase the stock quickly, though the number of flowers will be reduced, the plant using its energies to form fresh roots rather than in producing bloom. But the most important point is to provide a yearly mulch during early summer when the plants have finished flowering.

Of the hundred varieties known, some are believed to be extinct, some seem quite difficult to grow, whilst others are as easily managed as polyanthus and should form the basis of a beginner's collection. Of those that have a particularly strong perfume, Gerard's old double white, is still to be obtained and is a vigorous grower. Grown under cloches the blooms are ideal for bunching. Another Tudor primrose, Quaker's Bonnet, is also easy, the flowers being of a delightful pure lavender colour and possessing the true wild primrose perfume. Possibly the most vigorous grower is Marie Crousse, which covers itself with rich purple flowers, and are attractively edged with white. It was introduced from France about a hundred years ago and possesses easily the strongest perfume of all primroses being almost as powerful as the old red cabbage roses. Its perfume may be more accurately described as being like rose Tahiti, sweet and delicious. As charming as I find Sacheverell Sitwell's book on *Old Fashioned Flowers* to be, I cannot in any way agree with his description of Marie Crousse as being "not, in the writer's opinion, of outstanding interest". To my mind, it has everything, charm, rich perfume, a neat habit and a robust constitution. Of all the plants in my garden none is more appreciated.

A dainty little bloom is that of the old Irish variety, Red Paddy, which is very free flowering. The blooms are of a rich salmon-red shade, edged with white and possess a sweet fragrance. During the last year of the nineteenth century, the Cocker Brothers of Aberdeen, introduced about twenty new doubles, several of them most striking, but none more so than the deep rosy-pink flowered Bon Accord Elegans, whose flowers are flecked with creamy-white and are sweetly scented. This is now rare and though plants may still be obtained, they cost around two guineas. The variety Bon Accord Gem, which is rosy-lilac is almost as lovely, delicately fragrant, and much more easily grown. In this group we have the only real double blue primrose, Bon Accord Blue, which is of polyanthus habit and of a deep sky-blue colour; a really beautiful plant. As a contrast the lovely Bon Accord Purity, is most useful. The blooms are of a clear white, flushed green at the centre, giving it an icy appearance. Both varieties carry a rich woodland perfume.

Two other doubles to have a distinct perfume are Chevithorne Pink and Crathes Crimson. Both are plants of outstanding merit, the former bearing its pure shell-pink blooms on short sturdy polyanthus stems, their fragrance being delicate and sweet, whilst Crathes Crimson, is a rare and interesting primrose. It has a rich perfume and was found in the garden of Crathes Castle in Scotland. But what makes it more interesting is that it bears a flat bloom which has the familiar orange centre of the Bon Accord doubles and it would appear to be Bon Accord Crimson, thought to have been extinct for some time. To quote John Rea, once more, "it is a sweet and dainty flower and the chiefest of all our English kinds", which really does sum up this charming flower.

The fairy-like hose-in-hose or cup and saucer primroses are, if anything, even more attractive and they do all carry the delicate true primrose fragrance of the woodlands. This is Gerard's "double cowslip", one bloom growing out of the other, "like the breeches men do wear", said Parkinson in his *Paradisus* published in 1629. In this section, the old Irish Sparkler, is a beauty, producing tiny orange-red blooms, like the miniature polyanthus Fair Maid. Another is the primrose, apricot and pink shaded Lady Lettice, so valuable as an edging to a bed of bulbs for it blooms from early March right into June; whilst Brimstone, bears a clear sulphur-yellow bloom of perfect "hose" formation.

The Jack-in-the-Greens too, of polyanthus habit and with an attractive green ruff under each flower will, when better known, become popular for cutting. They may be obtained in a wide range of colours; white is the loveliest and I have yet to see a blue Jack.

My own collection of modern Juliae hybrids, so valuable for

rockeries and window-boxes consists of at least two hundred varieties, from the popular claret Wanda to the expensive Garryardes from Ireland, a new race of Juliae-type primroses which possess outstanding charm. Not only are the blooms large and the petals well formed, but they are held well above the foliage and possessing intense colouring are most striking and ideal subjects for a window-box, edging to a spring bedding display or on the rockery. They have a more distinct perfume than the other Juliae hybrids. Coming into bloom towards the end of March, a little earlier in the south, they have a long flowering season, often remaining in bloom until mid-May, nor do they lose their intense colouring as do many of the Wanda-type primroses. But I think their crowning glory is the attractive bronze-green foliage, and wine-red stems and though strong growing, the leaves are in no way coarse.

Last spring, I used the deep port-wine coloured variety, Hillhouse Red, to edge a bed of the white, Mrs. Krelage, daffodil and what an attractive show it made. This season I have planted the deep pink, Enid, amongst a drift of Muscari Heavenly Blue, a colour combination I saw in a friend's garden last April, planted beneath a tree of silver birch and the display was one of great beauty. Hillhouse Pink, is almost salmon coloured and Guinevere, an attractive shade of sea-shell pink. A variety of great charm is known as the Grail. The flowers are star-shaped and are a beautiful Elizabethan brick-red colour with a vivid orange eye. Another of merit is Victory, with its ruffled crimson-purple blooms and leaves of a cucumber green. An interesting variety with almost black flowers and unusual foliage of an apple green colour, veined red, is Sir Bedivere. The plants seem to be named after King Arthur and his times, by whom I do not know.

Perhaps the most striking of all the Garryardes is the 1954 introduction, Buckland primrose, which comes from Drake's old home in Devon. Try to imagine a huge ruffled bloom of rich creamy primrose colouring and flowering in profusion above a mass of red-bronze foliage and this is the new Buckland primrose.

Of the ordinary Juliae hybrids, I find that the lovely white variety, Craddock's White, possesses the most distinct fragrance, almost like ripe apples. This primrose is similar to the Garryardes in that it is of robust habit and its foliage is very deep green with a tinge of red in it. The bloom is of purest white.

These primroses will flourish with the minimum of manure, but they do like some humus and should be kept constantly damp about the roots. Like the doubles they are best moved early in July when the ground is moist.

Seed from both primroses and polyanthus is best sown immediately after it has ripened and been removed from the plants, which means the end of June or early July. Sow in a compost containing plenty of peat and some sand, in a cold frame or in boxes in the open which should be covered with a sheet of clean glass. I find that germination is quicker if the seed is not covered with compost, merely pressed into it. The seedlings should be pricked into boxes or into a cold frame during August where they are allowed to winter. If planted into beds early in March, they will soon come into bloom. For cutting, the strains of Messrs. Clucas, Read and Sutton's are excellent; for bedding, the large heads of plants raised from seed from the House of Blackmore and Langdon, especially their new pink, and from Toogoods are superb. But the best bed of polyanthus I have yet seen was raised from seed of the Hood River strain sent over from Oregon, U.S.A. The heads are immense, the colours breath-taking, from shell-pinks, through clear blues, to rich velvety cerise; the size of the individual pips measuring more than 1 inch across, the colour range being beyond the vision of the Victorian hybridists, Gertrude Jekyll and William Robinson, as valuable as their work has proved.

Quite distinct from our native garden auriculas are the lovely Alpine Auriculas, introduced to England by the Flemish weavers about the years 1580, and like so many of the quaint members of the primrose family, they are direct descendants from plants grown in Tudor gardens.

Parkinson, in his *Theatre of Plants*, calls them "Beares Ears" and named twenty-five varieties amongst them being such colours as ash, hair, and tawny. Some of them would undoubtedly be the native garden auricula. Popularity increased each year and by the mid-eighteenth century, named varieties having green and white edges appeared which were the forerunners of our modern alpine and exhibition or show auriculas. But soon an amazing change was to take place with a number of plants in the appearance of a white "paste", really due to the replacement of the petals by structures identical with that of the leaves. What we now know as the "show" auricula had arrived and interest in the alpine varieties possessing none of the fascinating "paste" rapidly declined. But today, the lovely golden-centred alpines, which except for those exhibiting require no glass to shield the blooms from rain as do the "paste" varieties, are making a come-back. Like the native garden auriculas they possess vigour and stamina to a far greater degree than the show varieties everlastingly grown in pots and under glass, and so may be grown in any cool position in the garden provided the soil is well cultivated. The alpines are ideal small garden plants and useful for a north border or position for the blooms are at their best when protected from strong sunlight. I think the present vogue of exhibiting, though stimulating interest in the auriculas has done much to make enthusiasts believe that it is a flower fit only for this purpose. But the alpine auricula is more vigorous and far happier in the garden than under glass, though I know old exhibitors will disagree with me. Treat them like the ordinary garden varieties and they will respond like magic, especially where given a position on a rockery where they may receive some shelter and protection by stones. Planted close to the stones, the blooms appear particularly beautiful. But wherever planted, the ground must be well drained and liberally enriched with leaf mould or peat, and some bone meal. Wet ground will only cause rotting of the thick rootstock. Planting should be done early in April, firmly but not too deeply. My own method is to remove offsets from the stock plants during late August, to pot these in $2\frac{1}{2}$-inch pots and stand in a cold frame until the following April where they may then be planted in the open ground. Use plenty of peat in the potting compost, a little sand, and some crushed charcoal to keep the soil sweet. As plants of alpines are always more expensive than the garden auriculas, a stock may be commenced by sowing seed and although the known named varieties will not come true, you may be lucky enough to obtain one or two choice plants, and others that will be of value for outdoor planting. The seed should be obtained in a fresh condition, as soon as it is really ripe and it should be sown at once. This will be about the end of July. Sow in pans in a cold frame or greenhouse in a John Innes seed compost and just press the seeds into it without covering them in any way. Cover the pan with a sheet of glass and provided the weather is warm, germination should not be long delayed.

The alpine section may be divided into two classes, those blooms having a gold centre and those with a white centre. All are fragrant, but outstandingly so are Mrs. Hearn, pale blue with a white centre; Mrs. Florence Levy, which has an almost black petal, ringed with scarlet and edged apricot and a golden centre. Another of outstanding fragrance is Basuto, with bright crimson petals and a gold centre; whilst Golden Chalice, has a golden centre of perfect form and a body colour of rich golden-bronze.

In the white section, Argus is robust and has a petal of a contrasting rich plum-colour; whilst Blue Bonnet has petals of intense violet-blue, richly perfumed.

Like the garden auriculas, they will bloom late in spring when the single and double primroses are finishing, and they will prolong the season until the end of May.

Of the delightful garden auriculas, plants native to England, three varieties possess outstanding fragrance with Celtic King perhaps the loveliest of all auriculas for the garden. The blooms are pale lemon-yellow with extremely frilled petals which carry a powerful lemon perfume. The purple-blue variety, Blue Velvet, with a white centre, a robust grower is also strongly fragrant, so too is that choice terra-cotta flowered variety, Southport. Of the Old Dusty Millers, though quaint, I can detect no perfume.

For the rockery, trough garden and alpine house, the little *Primula pubescens* is a plant possessing real charm. Not all the varieties are scented, though possibly the two best varieties carry a rich, sweet perfume. One, Mrs. Wilson, bears a large bloom on a 4-inch stem of rich lilac with a striking white centre; the other, Faldonside, bears a small bloom of richest velvety-crimson on 3-inch stems. They are charming plants for pots or bowls in the home, for they remain long in bloom and distil their perfume over a wide area.

CHAPTER V

VIOLETS AND VIOLAS

NATIVE, not only to Britain but to almost all countries of the world, the sweet scented violet, *Viola odorata*, was one of the greatest of childhood pleasures. So shy to reveal its dainty blooms there was always great excitement whenever we came upon them in woodland or hedgerow. The primrose was more readily seen for its brightly coloured blooms and leaves attracted immediate attention even when growing in grass, but one had to seek out the violet, for it clustered around the roots of hawthorn hedge and woodland trees and its small dark leaves and even smaller and darker blooms scarcely revealed themselves to our young eyes. To be able to pick a bunch of the blooms was considered a great feat and they were carefully placed in a tiny vase of water and treasured until they died.

As with the wild thyme, the writers of old connected the violet with its ability to provide sound sleep and for those who found sleep difficult to come by were advised to bind the fresh blooms of violets round their foreheads and temples and sleep would overtake one almost immediately. A pleasant fragrant perfume no matter of what flower will encourage one to relax, when sleep will soon follow. Until the beginning of the twentieth century, people knew how to relax, and to bring fragrance to their senses the utmost use was made of dried herbs, pot-pourri, sweet bags of lavender and geranium leaves, and those delightful oranges stuck with cloves. The violet was much used for drying the blooms for filling muslin bags for hanging about the bedroom; or for placing amongst clothes and bedding and Conserve of Violets was also much used "for inflammation in children" or "to cool a burning fever" as the mid-seventeenth-century *Gentlewoman's Companion* tells us. For these reasons the violet became as popular in the herb garden as did the rose and lily, also similarly used in the household.

Today the violet is to be seen in few gardens other than where grown commercially in Dorset, Devon and Cornwall. We now only appreciate size and blatant colour, though the revival of the primrose may also signify a welcome return to these quaint and fragrant plants so beloved in olden times.

Violets love partial shade and so may be planted anywhere in the garden. They will be quite happy in a shrubbery provided the soil is not sour and impoverished, but I always feel that their freedom of flowering is to be enjoyed to the full when they are given a bed to themselves but in a position away from the hot summer sun and sheltered from the prevailing spring winds. The best time for planting the rooted runners is the last fortnight of May but first the soil must be well worked. Being moisture loving plants, a soil containing plenty of humus is essential. A heavy loam, to which has been added as much humus as possible is ideal. Well rotted manure is generally out of the question but some old mushroom bed compost can often be found, or peat mixed with straw or chaff rotted down with an activator is equally valuable. Those like myself, living on the coast, can use seaweed with advantage. Spent hops too are useful and of course, leaf mould. As violets do not like an acid soil, some lime should be added to correct any acidity. Just as important as the preparation of the soil is to plant in as sheltered a position as possible.

No flowers are happy which have to endure continuous buffeting from spring winds. Where the shelter of a wall is not available, wattle hurdles may be used as a wind-break, whilst owing to its density almost to ground level, I find 3-ft. beech hedging very suitable. This will also provide some shade.

The runners should be purchased from a reliable source and before planting should be dipped in a nicotine-soft-soap solution to protect against the violet's chief enemy, aphis. The long jointed, straggling type of runner should not be planted. Where possible plant during a wet period and until the plants become established it is vital to see that they do not suffer from dry conditions. Set out the plants about 12 inches apart keeping in mind that for early bloom some form of covering may be used during winter. My own method is to use 4-ft. lights and to plant in beds allowing 10 inches between the rows. During summer, all runners should be systematically removed from the plants for it is essential to build up a strong crown which can devote all its energies to producing bloom. During August, some dry soot should be worked in between the rows and the plants given a weekly application of manure water. A dressing of equal parts bone meal and sulphate of potash given at the rate of 2 oz. per square yard and raked well in will prove of value. The ground must also be kept clean by the constant use of the hoe throughout summer. It cannot be emphasised too much that the early spring crop of bloom will depend entirely on the cultivations during a previous summer. Spraying the plants against red spider and aphis is also necessary. Red Spider, which is generally only troublesome during dry, hot weather is controlled by the use of a white petroleum oil emulsion, and aphis by a nicotine and soft soap solution.

The beds should be covered during late October when they will soon begin to give some bloom and they may be left covered until April 1st when the lights will be required elsewhere. At all times, strict attention must be made to watering and ventilation, for a too close atmosphere and excess moisture hanging about the plants will cause mildew with the rotting of the buds or spotting of the blooms. If the frames are shaded during periods of strong sunlight, the plants will require almost no watering throughout winter.

The two best violets for providing masses of bloom are the vigorous, sweetly-scented Princess of Wales and the hardy, Governor Herrick, which is resistant to red spider and drought though its almost complete lack of perfume might prevent its admission to our garden of scented plants.

The Parma violets are not sufficiently hardy for growing away from the south-west but there is always a demand for plants of the other delightfully coloured varieties, the hardy reddish-purple Admiral Avellan; the double mauve, and less hardy, Marie Louise, and its white counterpart, Comte de Brazza; the delightful rose-pink, Cœur d'Alsace; and the unusual creamy-buff coloured, Sulphurea. The variety, White Czar, possesses a sweet perfume as does the reddish-flowered Czar, still grown commercially and is one of the neatest plants for planting in the orchard or woodland garden for only there will the quaint shyness of the violet be appreciated, as it was during childhood days, and only there will the blooms carry that sweet perfume of the woodlands that we love so much in spring.

Wedded to the sweet scented violet is the pansy and viola, and all those dainty violettas and species which are now so popular for bedding and for rockery planting. Like the primrose, almost every variety may be said to possess at least a faint fragrance though others are more heavily blessed with scent. Of the many excellent strains of pansies available today, that possessing the most perfume is Read's New Century Scented strain. The blooms are large, of superb colouring and they carry a rich, sweet perfume. Love-in-idleness and Heart's Ease was the name given to pansies by the writers of old; what delightful names they were, reminders of idle hours in the early summer sun, those boyhood days when with not a care in the world those big beds of pansies of our grandparents were always a matter of interest, when there was no one about to play any cricket. Each bloom seemed to possess a different "face", some were like cats, others were blotched giving the appearance of owls' faces and we tried to think of something different for every one.

Pansies do best if sown under cloches in August or in a cold frame and will come into bloom in early summer if planted out in early April and they do love a soil containing plenty of humus by way of peat or decayed leaves. If sown in March, the plants will not be in bloom until much later in the summer.

Whilst pansies are grown almost entirely from seed except those show pansies, so beloved by Victorian gardeners for exhibition, violas are generally propagated from base cuttings taken in August and rooted in frames of sandy soil, or better still in a mixture of sand and peat. Of neater habit, violas are today preferred for bedding and from the many varieties available, a few may be said to possess a definite perfume. The old variety, Maggie Mott, early and most free flowering is richly scented, so is the charming new fuchsia-pink variety, Doris. The lovely compact, Chantryland, is also sweetly perfumed, the rich apricot colour of its dainty blooms being most attractive too. That grand viola, H. H. Hodge, with its lemon-coloured bloom edged with lavender-blue is also fragrant.

Nor must we leave out of our gardens those charming little violettas which carry the mild scent of the woodlands. The reddish-purple Lady Sackville, has quite a strong perfume, so has the creamy-white flowered, Little David. The lovely pale mauve, Queen of the Year, has a slight fragrance. There are others and all are delightful subjects for the rockery and window-box.

There is another race of violas, all of which carry a sweet fragrance and these flower throughout the winter and so are dealt with in the chapter on Winter Fragrance.

CHAPTER VI

SCENTED ANNUALS AND BIENNIALS

FOR filling in gaps in the border, for sowing round the garden house and in any odd corners under a window or about an entrance door, annuals and biennials are more than useful, particularly those which carry perfume. There is nothing more deliciously scented than clumps of mignonette, *Nicotiana* and night-scented stocks used with abandon about the garden, which is the only way to sow most annuals. Sweet peas, may be an exception, but this summer quite apart from those long rows of exhibition blooms which from mid-July perfume every room in the house, we have planted them along wattle hurdle fencing and have trained them up rustic poles and even up the bare lower stems of virginia creeper and ivy which clothe the upper walls of the house. Now the walls are clothed right down to the ground and how charming they look and what delicious fragrance steeps through the windows, especially from a packet of American hybrids which possess a stronger perfume than any sweet-peas I have ever grown.

Of the wide variety of these delightful old fashioned annuals and biennials none conveys the true cottage charm better than the sweet-william. They are so easy to grow from seed and make such a brilliant show of colour that they should be in every garden. It has all the good points of a top class cut flower and none of the bad ones. It is clean, blooms profusely, has a most charming perfume, lasts a considerable time in water and what is most important to the housewife, does not shed its petals about the house. No wonder then that it has now become so popular again. The sweet-william is really perennial, but is generally treated as a biennial, thus it does not become too straggly in the border. For my part I have always treated the plant as perennial and have allowed beds to remain down for many years with no deterioration of size or colour of the blooms.

Propagation is from seed sown in the open ground in the south or in cold frames in the north. April is the best month. The tiny seed should be mixed with dry, coarse sand before sowing so as not to sow too thickly. The seedlings must be transplanted to beds 9 inches apart before they are allowed to become too drawn in the rows. Of all nursery plants it is the sweet-william which is generally sold in a wretched long lanky condition from which it never recovers. This can be guarded against by early transplanting. The plant is not too particular as to soil conditions but I do think the blooms take on a more brilliant tone if the plants are set out in a loamy soil which has been slightly manured for a previous crop; and they do love lime. There are three popular self colours and the well known Auricula-eyed strain. Of the selfs there is Giant White, Scarlet Beauty, and the most popular Pink Beauty which is a glorious salmon-pink. Planted in clumps about the herbaceous border they are delightful.

Then there is Dianthus Delight. This is yet another crossing of sweet wivelsfield with an alpine form, the result being a hardy annual of a most wonderful colour range. Growing to a height of only 8 inches it is an ideal plant for filling up spaces in the rockery left vacant by those plants which have failed to survive the winter months. It is also a most useful plant for filling up spaces at the front of a border. The individual blooms borne in great profusion may be likened to a large sweet-william though the colour range is wider. For an early display, seed should be sown in gentle heat in early February and the seedlings hardened off in cold frames before being planted in the open some time in April, depending upon weather conditions.

Another lovely annual or biennial introduced to England two centuries ago is *Dianthus Chinensis*. Details of cultivation are the same as described for Dianthus Delight, but the taller growing plant is generally used for cutting or in the border as in some instances it can be seen growing to a height of nearly 2 ft. As with all dianthus, only very gentle heat should be employed for the seed sowing and as soon as the seedlings appear, plenty of fresh air should be given. In the north, it may be better to treat the plant as a biennial, sowing the seed in late July in cold frames or the open ground. There are several excellent named varieties, the best being the vivid single red, Crimson Belle; Fireball, brilliant double scarlet; Salmon Queen, a lovely fringed single salmon, and, The Bride, a single white with a crimson eye.

The Marguerite carnation, is a cross of the *Chinensis* with a border strain. As an annual it deserves to be more widely known for it is an excellent cut flower, has attractive double frilled blooms and comes into bloom less than six months from the time the seed is sown and possesses an attractive perfume.

A delightful new annual dianthus is called Pink Bedder, a Coronation Year novelty from the House of Allwood. From July until well into October it produces a mass of rich salmon-pink flowers, which are superb when planted in beds to them-selves. If the seed is sown in heat early in March the plants will by mid-summer have made bushy growth and will soon be smothered with their attractively sweet scented flowers. Growing to a height of about 10 inches this makes a pleasant companion to the now established Red Bedder, described by the late C. H. Middleton, as being easily the best red bedding plant for summer. It is of similar habit and very free flowering though not quite so sweetly perfumed.

Though the wallflower is a spring flower it is almost always treated as a biennial and so we must inhale the richness of its perfume in this chapter. Really it is a perennial and is frequently seen growing as such in old Elizabethan brick walls, but used for bedding it tends to become rather straggling if left for a second season whilst the blooms become small and seem to lose their perfume. Parkinson tells us from his *Paradisus* that "the sweetness of the flowers causeth them to be generally used in nosegayes", and he tells us that their distillation "is used for a remedy for the palsy". In the *Paradisus* he gives a picture of the "great double red wallflower" which is now only occasionally seen in gardens, though the singles we know so well. It is still possible to

D

obtain seed of double brown and double yellow, the plants being of dwarf habit and the flowers possessing a heavy fragrance.

Though so useful for inter-planting with tall Cottage or Darwin tulips, the yellow shades looking most attractive when planted with purple tulips, it is when massed in raised beds that the wallflower is seen at its best using two or three colours which are planted in circles or in rows of self colours. Most colourful and fragrant in this way is White Dame, when planted as a centre piece, surrounded by the vivid Scarlet Emperor, which in turn is bordered by the rich, deep yellow, Golden Monarch. Such a bed will remain a mass of colour for almost two months and provide plenty of bloom for cutting for the home. The old gardeners would place sprays of the blooms in saucers of water about the bedroom where its fragrance would bring about peaceful sleep. But it is equally restful to grow this plant in beds beneath a cottage window with apple blossom overhanging, especially the blossom of that grand cooking apple Arthur Turner, so beautifully scented. After an early summer shower during late afternoon with a gentle breeze blowing from the Quantocks, a Somerset cottage must be heaven on earth. But we all tend to sow our wallflower seed too late and when we do sow early, we allow the plants to remain in the seed rows until they have formed top roots, which will make them difficult to transplant. Sow the seed thinly early in May and transplant to beds as soon as large enough to handle. There they will make bushy plants during summer and may be moved to their permanent quarters in October.

The Cheiranthus or Siberian wallflower, which blooms later, during early and into mid-summer, and though possessing only a delicate perfume in comparison with the old blood-red wallflower, is an indispensable plant for the herbaceous border, providing brilliant colouring when there is little other colour. Besides the deep orange coloured *C. allionii*, Golden Bedder bears bright golden-yellow flowers and is equally attractive. Plant with it the intense Oxford-blue flowered clary, *Salvia harminum*, which is one of the most striking biennials in the herbaceous border. Like all the sages it is delightfully aromatic.

It grows readily from seed sown in early summer when it will bloom the following year.

It is good to see the sweet-scented mignonette (*Reseda odorata*) coming back to favour. Up to the early 1930s it was a plant to be found in all cottage gardens and its delicious perfume could be detected by anyone leaning over the garden gate. But the sombre coloured blooms had to give way to flowers of more brilliant colouring like the greatly improved zinnia and the antirrhinum and nemesia and until very recently it seemed almost lost to our gardens. It is surprising how the demand is always for colour and size rather than for perfume and flavour. It is the same with fruit. From a seed sowing in late March, the plants will come into bloom by midsummer and continue until late in autumn. There are a number of varieties, the sweet-scented which is highly fragrant, and Golden Goliath, which bears a large deep golden-yellow bloom are both delightful plants. The Machet form of which there are several varieties and which bear fine broad spikes of copperyred flowers are also extremely sweetly perfumed. Of these, Rubin, is possibly the best variety, but even more robust and fragrant is Hurst's new Red Monarch.

But as lovely as are the mignonettes in the garden, their fragrance is more appreciated indoors during winter. This is possible if seed is sown early in September in pans or pots containing a compost made up of loam, sand and peat. The 60 size pots are best and two or three seeds should be sown in the centre of each. As soon as germination has taken place, the seedlings should be reduced to a single plant which is stopped when 4 inches tall. Water only when really necessary, otherwise the plants may damp off, and stand in a light room in a temperature of about 50° F. Your friends will be amazed at the glorious New Year fragrance of one's rooms, a breath of the old cottage garden during winter. The richly scented East Lothian stocks, or Intermediate stocks, as they are sometimes called also make ideal indoor pot plants. This is a strain of sweetly fragrant plants which if sown in small pots in late July will come into bloom in a warm greenhouse early in spring, or if sown outdoors will bloom late in summer. The best method of cultivation is to sow the seed outdoors in drills. Brompton stocks may also be sown in the same way and to transplant into individual pots early in September for spring flowering indoors. Those required for outdoor bedding may in sheltered gardens be transplanted to permanent beds in September, but in cold, exposed districts they are better wintered in the rows under cloches and transplanted early in spring.

Intermediate stocks may be obtained in all colours, so may the Bromptons, but in this section three are outstanding, Queen Astrid, brightest crimson; Empress Elizabeth, bright rose-pink; and the clear mauve, Lavender Lady.

The stocks most of us know so well are annuals, called ten-week stocks, on account of their flowering period from early July until mid-September. They may be planted in clumps about a border, but are at their loveliest when in beds. They could well be used more often in gardens for the blind for if long narrow beds are made alongside a path the fragrance of the flowers will be appreciated to the full. I have vivid recollections of taking an almost blind person through a garden in which grew beds of stocks. Few words were spoken until coming near to the beds of these richly perfumed plants, and then "Oh, the stocks, how lovely." Their fragrance was unmistakable even midst a garden full of fragrant plants.

Sow them in early March in gentle heat or later in the month in a cold frame and keep them as dry as possible throughout their life for they so easily "damp off" and as they are not quite hardy, do not plant them out until the end of May, or until frosts have disappeared for a few months. Only by obtaining a good strain of seed can a high degree of double flowered plants be expected and try a few of the more unusual colours, apple blossom, canary-yellow, flesh, copper, crimson, pansy-purple, and you will be delightfully surprised.

I always like plenty of sweet alyssum in my garden and wherever possible use it for edging. Eleanour Sinclair Rohde, that great authority on herbs and sweet smelling plants describes its perfume as being like that of new-mown hay. Its fragrance really does remind one of the stack yard which adjoins my garden, though my small son says it smells just like honeycomb which may be nearer to it. In any case, it must be picked for its fragrance to be enjoyed, or one may bend down and breathe in its freshness. But for all that, it is a friendly little plant, so easily grown and I like the way it spreads itself during mid-summer like an old hen protecting her chickens. By early August plants 10 inches apart will touch each other and smother themselves in blooms of violet or of purest white. They are one of the few plants that can be mixed with roses and form a delightful edging to a rose bed, especially is the white, Little Dorrit, most attractive, used as an edging to a bed of the crimson Ena Harkness rose. The richly coloured Violet Queen is also charming for edging. The seed is sown in gentle heat in March, the seedlings being pricked off into boxes when large enough and the plants go into the open ground in May.

For covering a bank or a dry sunny corner where few other plants will survive, the nasturtium grows vigorous and blooms prolific. It is the new Gleam Hybrids that are sweetly scented but they need to be smelt in the hand and not from afar, for though pleasantly sweet their perfume is very delicate. One possessing rather more perfume than the others is the new Fiery Festival, which bears semi-double flowers of Paul Crampel geranium colour, and is of compact habit. Another is Primrose Gleam, bearing rich lemon-yellow flowers, whilst Moon Gleam, is of the palest shade of cream. The variety, Delightful, bears blooms of a soft shade of salmon which possess a very sweet fragrance. Sow the seed in a dry soil of a poor nature, like that of most shrubberies, for in a rich loam the plants make leaf at the expense of bloom, and today the leaf of the nasturtium is not appreciated for mixing with salads, nor is it "given to children for the worms" as Parkinson writes.

During boyhood days most cottagers pickled nasturtium seeds, they were as one of the old writers says "hot and bitter", but with bread and cheese they were just the thing for refreshment at the end of a long tramp over the moors, washed down with elderberry wine. Those who appreciate a savoury taste will enjoy the leaves placed with those of lettuce between brown bread with grated cheese and a covering of salad cream.

Or as Parkinson tells us "mixed with Tarrogon or Rocket, they are savoury to some men's stomach". I have not tried Rocket, but with chopped chives they make an appetising meal for a chilly day.

Bacon mentions the French marigold as being fragrant, but only the true *Tagetes signata*, seems to carry scent, the French marigold, *Tagetes patula*, possessing no more than a slight aromatic freshness. *Tagetes signata*, is a hardy annual which forms neat round bush-like plants growing to a height of only 8 inches and is as round as it is tall. From early June until the autumn it covers itself with small yellow star-shaped blooms, which are most attractive growing amidst the dark green feathery foliage. They possess a refreshing lemon perfume and are lovely when planted with nemesia, or the sapphire-blue Lobelia, and backed by antirrhinums. The two best varieties are Golden Gem, pale yellow; and Golden Ring, which bears deep orange coloured flowers.

Does the calendula, the Pot marigold possess flavour? The foliage seems to carry an aromatic perfume which is quite pleasant but there is almost no perfume in the blooms though many of the older writers thought there was. Parkinson describes the Great Garden marigold, and of its value in the herb rather than in the flower garden. "As a comforter of the heart and spirits," he writes and "The syrupe, made of the fresh flowers, are used to the same purposes to good effect". Today we give the calendula the usual hardy annual treatment and use it entirely in the flower garden where it is colourful and blooming over a long period. Here is much bloom for cutting for indoor decoration. There are many strains and varieties, but outstanding is the orange quilled Radio, and its yellow counterpart, Golden Beam. The variety Market Tangerine, is rich in colour and Apricot Queen, an unusual shade of apricot-orange.

A hardy annual which has never been allowed to lose popularity is *Iberis odorata*, the sweet scented candytuft, one of the loveliest of all annuals for the flat blooms are obtained in shades of white, pink, lilac and crimson, and carry a faint but delightful, almost woodland perfume, whilst they are extremely long flowering. One of the loveliest of all is Dobbie's

Spiral, which bears pure white heads of richly scented flowers. As a contrast, the rosy-scarlet, Rose Cardinal, of compact habit is free flowering over a long period. Like most other hardy annuals the seed may be sown about the border or in small beds in any part of the garden though the candytuft does appreciate a deeply worked soil.

A little-known plant which is an annual and a great favourite of bees is *Limnanthes*, a dwarf plant found in its natural state growing amongst the rocks in parts of Nevada and California. It is extremely free flowering, delightfully scented, almost like white clover and covers itself with tiny yellow and white flowers throughout summer from an early April sowing. It is a refreshing little plant which does well in almost any position and in any ordinary soil.

One of my earliest recollections is of a trellis covered with thousands of blooms of the old-fashioned sweet-pea, not the refined hybrid we know today, but those small white and carmine-red flowers borne on thin little stems and yet what perfume they carried. It was delicious, almost "thick" like the perfume of honeysuckle or Ena Harkness rose, and it seemed to scent the whole garden. The seed was sown in September and by early summer the trellis was covered to the top with fragrant blooms. It is rarely seen today and few catalogues seem to list it. This is an age of sophistication in the garden, and so the large flowered hybrids take pride of place, many carrying almost no perfume it is sad to say, for the trend with our hybridists is to concentrate on size and colour in all flowers and fruits. Even so, the modern sweet-pea is indispensable to the garden for it is one of the most valuable of all summer flowers for cutting, one of its great qualities being its tremendous freedom in flowering. Seed sown under cloches or in a cold frame in August, where they will remain over winter, may be planted outside in early April and will come into bloom early in June. Or the seed may be sown in gentle heat in February, the young plants being stopped when 2 inches tall, transferred to a frame in early April and set out in the open at the month end. Or the seed may be sown where the plants are to bloom and if sown in early April the plants will come into bloom early in August. To ensure rapid and even germination, the seed of hard-skinned varieties should be chipped with a sharp knife on the side opposite the "eye". Such varieties are Margaret O'Brien, Elizabeth Taylor, Carlotta, Reconnaissance, Red Velvet, Warrior, Viola and The Clown, all exhibition favourites.

To get those thick long stems and four large blooms on each which is the hall-mark of an exhibition sweet-pea, they must be done well. They like a soil which has been enriched with decayed manure and some peat to keep the soil cool and moist for the plants must be grown in a position of full sun and this may mean dry conditions. But the best sweet-peas always seem to be grown in a sandwich of decayed garden refuse, soil, manure and lime. A trench is made during early November and at the bottom is placed a thick layer of pea haulm, potato tops, lettuces that have gone to seed, anything in fact that is the remains of the vegetable garden. This is allowed to settle for a fortnight, then a 2 inch layer of soil is placed on top and trodden down. A layer of decayed manure follows, then more soil and finally a good dusting with lime. Like the culinary pea, sweet-peas are great lime lovers which seems to bring out the colour of the blooms. With each layer of soil is scattered some peat. The operation will possibly take all winter to complete, but the effort will be well worth while.

All sweet peas possess some fragrance but certain varieties are blessed with exceptional perfume and some of the best are:

RED SHADES

Air Warden.   Quite the best orange-scarlet. The flowers are sun-proof, sweetly scented and the plant is of robust habit.

Red Velvet.   A recent Unwin introduction, the colour being deep blood-crimson. The blooms are quite sunproof and retain their colour and fragrance when cut.

PINK AND ROSE SHADES

Mollie.   Rich deep cerise-pink long stemmed and large flowered.

Monty.   Clear shell-pink with a white base. The blooms are large and sweetly scented.

Pink Opal. This is a robust grower. The blooms are of orchid-pink on an amber ground, the petals being frilled and well formed and carrying a rich perfume.

SALMON SHADES

Betty. One of the finest of all sweet-peas, the colour is rich cherry, flushed salmon-pink, the petals having an attractive golden base.

Leicester. The huge blooms are of a warm shade of salmon-pink, delightfully frilled and long stemmed.

LAVENDER AND MAUVE SHADES

Elizabeth Taylor. The huge frilled flowers are carried on long sturdy stems. The colour is deep mauve.

Mrs. C. Kay. Now well established as one of the best of its class as a clear lavender-blue.

Purple Velvet. The best deep purple though not so fragrant as Elizabeth Taylor.

BLUE SHADES

Blue Bell. An old established variety of rich perfume and of a brilliant bluebell-blue colour.

Myosotis. Sweetly scented and one of the finest of all sweet-peas, the colour being rich mid-blue, the petals being wavy and carried on long stems.

CREAM AND WHITE SHADES

Albatross. The finest of all whites, the huge blooms being borne on stout stems. Of purest white they are richly perfumed.

Cream Gigantic. The large frilled blooms are of a rich cream colour and are possibly the most richly scented of all sweet-peas.

Moonlight. Off-white would best describe this magnificent variety, the blooms being large and beautifully frilled.

These fragrant sweet-peas could well be used more often trained up trellis or canes against the side of a house. How charming they look against a whitewashed cottage, especially the more colourful reds and blues. Or trained up stout twiggy sticks they make an admirable "hedge" possibly to give privacy to one's garden or to divide the herb or vegetable plot from the flower garden. The trend is to grow them mainly for exhibition or for shop sale with the result that our gardens miss much of their charm and fragrance. Used to grow up circular 6-ft. tall netting or canes which are planted about the back of the herbaceous border or alongside a path or drive, their perfume will be appreciated; they will be colourful too and always provide some bloom for cutting for the home for a more pleasing perfume in the house is difficult to equal.

CHAPTER VII

THE HERBACEOUS BORDER

DISAPPOINTING it is to those who love perfume in plants to find that so few of those plants which have been improved out of all recognition during recent years and which have become the most popular plants of the border possess no perfume at all. I am thinking of those stately delphiniums, the colourful lupin and michaelmas daisies, the phlox; even the old world peony has lost much of its perfume, as indeed have many of the modern varieties. That lush fragrance seems to have departed from the garden of today compared with most of the old world gardens of childhood days when those huge cabbage-like pink and red peonies and clumps of catmint and other herbs made the garden not only a thing of beauty, but a place where one could go to be refreshed, for a garden which does not fulfil all that it was originally intended to do is only half a garden. By all means plant some of those wonderful new hybrid plants, but let them rub leaves with those possessing richness of perfume.

Where possible, the herbaceous border should be in a sheltered place, beneath an old garden wall where strong winds are almost excluded and one is able to enjoy the perfume of the plants to the full. Or failing this, a row of 5-ft. wattle hurdles will give protection and act as a pleasing background. And have a path alongside the border, either of grass or of crazy paving planted with camomile which when trodden upon will exhale its delicate fragrance.

One fequently hears the herbaceous border condemned by modern gardeners as demanding far too much of their time in staking and weeding round plants which may be left down for several years and which gradually become entwined with perennial weeds. There is some foundation for both these claims but surely there is nothing in the garden more attractive than a well-stocked herbaceous border, which will provide colour from May until November. And if sufficient shelter is provided it is possible to dispense with staking almost entirely if the delphinium is left out of the scheme and the wall or hurdles are covered by fragrant climbing roses, such as we see in those delightful Elizabethan gardens of which England is justly proud.

But no herbaceous plant will do well in a weed infested, impoverished soil. They are gross feeders and humus by way of well rotted manure, horticultural peat, decayed leaves or composted straw must be dug in and the ground cleared of all perennial weeds. October is the best month for this work, after which the ground should be allowed several weeks to settle down again before planting at the month end or early in November. This in most areas is the ideal planting time, for the plants will have begun to form new roots before the severe weather of January and February and will give a pleasing display their first summer, which they will not do if planted in March.

The herbaceous border should be planted with those plants best suited to the size of the garden. A small town garden for instance, should be planted with lilies-of-the-valley and other fragrant lilies, with bergamot and pinks, sweet-williams and scented violas; plants which are of compact habit. Violas or pinks may be used for an edging instead of the long flowered catmint which is so enchanting as an edging to a large border.

In an old garden that I had before the war, the herbaceous border terminated at a 5-ft. box hedge, through which was a small opening leading into a tiny herb garden, where also grew violets and the wild yellow primrose. One could enjoy the sweet scents of the peonies and pinks and the evening primroses, and then the aromatic fragrance of the herbs, so pronounced after a summer shower. Perhaps it may be possible to make the herb garden as a continuation of the border, divided by a hedge of lavender or rosemary. Or where space is limited, the bush herbs could be incorporated into the border, the sages planted with the purple-flowered garden salvias, the lavenders with the tall regal lilies. The border would then remain colourful and evergreen all the year round and would also provide both flowers and herbs for the home. This is the border planted in Tudor gardens, a combination of beauty and of value. It was of these late Tudor gardens that Harrison wrote in his *Description of England* about the year 1580. "If you look into our gardens . . . how wonderfully is their beauty increased, not only with flowers, but with rare and medicinal herbs". And this combination to my mind is gardening at its best, for a garden then becomes alive and is a thing of continuous interest throughout the year.

The first of the plants suitable for the herbaceous border is the charming and sweetly perfumed lily-of-the-valley, *Convallaria majalis*, about which the mediaeval poet Montgomery wrote "I love the lily as the first of flowers", possibly meaning that the lily was the first of summer flowers or that it was first in his affections. This lovely plant is happiest in the dappled shade enjoyed by the primrose and violet, indeed like those flowers it is a native of the woodlands, where it enjoys the moist, humus laden soil it loves so well. Where it is seen in most gardens it has been planted in the sour soil of a shrubbery where it receives the minimum amount of sunlight and air and has a soil almost devoid of humus. And so we rarely see it at its best, which it will be if planted in the border, in a soil containing some peat and decayed manure and where its roots may enjoy the coolness provided by the partial shade of its neighbouring plants. The crowns should be planted in late autumn, spacing them 6 inches apart so that they do not become too crowded and what is so important, they should be given a mulch with leaf mould or peat during autumn of every year.

A plant very similar with its milky-white bells and glossy dark green foliage and which requires almost identical culture is the quaint old world Solomon's seal, so useful for cutting during early summer. Like the lily-of-the-valley it thrives in a cool, moist soil which brings out the unusual heavy fragrance of the flowers. If planted near clumps of lilies-of-the-valley, its long arching sprays provide the lilies with protection from strong sunlight. Of this plant, Robinson tell us in *The English Flower Garden* that there are twenty-three species known, but that most familiar to English gardens is *Polygonatum multiflorum*, which is hardy and free flowering. Like the lily-of-the-valley the plant may be grown in the wild or woodland garden, planted with bluebells and primroses and fragrant daffodils, which may be allowed to remain untouched for years, their craving for humus and a moist, cool soil being provided by the constant shedding of the leaves of the trees. Solomon's seal, is a plant native to our shores and was grown in olden times for its value in taking away bruises, the freshly dug root being applied to the skin.

Also suited to the wild garden and the border is that lovely pale yellow flowering plant the evening primrose, now alas, only occasionally seen in our gardens. In my grandfather's garden, where grew the biennial species, *Oenothera biennis Lamarckiana*, which bears its richly perfumed flowers throughout summer, at their sweetest and brightest during early evening when the hot sun has gone down, these lovely plants seeded themselves in abundance and always in early autumn he would dig up a number for me to plant in my garden where they always looked charming, but where they never seeded themselves in anything like the number in the rich loam of his garden. They should be planted to the back of a border, for they often grow 5 ft. tall. Several of the perennial species of the *Oenothera* possess a rich perfume, particularly *O. marginata*, which grows only 10-12 inches tall and covers itself with white, shaded pale rose blooms during May and early June, which retain their beauty throughout the night emitting, as Robinson tells us "a magnolia-like odour". This is a delightful plant for an edging to the border for it is of neat habit and possesses attractive, almost holly-like leaves in addition to its scent.

June is the month of the lush peony, the peony-rose as it is always called in Ireland, of all flowers it is the one that appears equally at home in the garden of castle or cottage. It is of an exotic nature, several of the double flowered varieties carrying the rich thick perfume of the Orient, from where they reached Europe early in the sixteenth century. These are the *Paeonia Chinensis* hybrids, but the European species, *P. officinalis*, which was known to our gardens much earlier is at its best during the latter half of May, thus extending the flowering season from mid-May until the end of July. It is only the Chinese species which possesses perfume in certain varieties and as charming as are their European cousins, they do not come under the scope of the fragrant border.

When once established, peonies should be left undisturbed for almost a lifetime, which is the secret of those mammoth clumps of rich green foliage carrying a mass of buds seen only in old world gardens. For this reason, they must be planted in a soil containing plenty of humus in the form of decayed manure and leaf mould which was the secret of success in the cottage gardens of old. The finest peonies I ever saw were growing in a border entirely to themselves in the garden of an old farmhouse in Shropshire. Upon asking the secret of their magnificence the farmer said that whenever there was a spare barrow load of manure available, it was spread over the peonies during autumn and again as a summer mulch around the crowns in early May. The farmer's wife very kindly cut me a large bunch of buds just showing the pale pink of the fragrant variety, Sarah Bernhardt, which remained colourful and fragrant in our home for fully three weeks. The ability of the buds to open fully when cut is one of the valuable characteristics of the peony, for indoors as well as out, its beauty and fragrance may be enjoyed over a longer period than any other herbaceous flower. It is the cream and pink shades which are most fragrant, possessing as my son, William, says "the scent of face cream", which is as near as their fragrance could possibly be described and have not the women of China, where the plant has been cultivated since the beginning of time, washed their faces in water into which peonies have been placed.

September and October are the months when the peony is dormant and this is the best planting time. Another secret of success is shallow planting, for the eyes should be covered with not more than 2 inches of soil. The plants should also be given plenty of room for they will grow into bushes rather than plants when established. Besides the pink and silver blooms of Sarah Bernhardt, others possessing the same unique fragrance are:

Couronne d'Or. White and unique in that the petals are laced with crimson.

Duchess de Nemours. Early, and bearing blooms of purest white shaded cream at the centre.

Festiva Maxima. Which bears huge white flowers, flecked with crimson and which is one of the earliest to bloom.

Karl Rosenfield. The most fragrant of all the crimson-reds and the strongest grower.

Lady Alexander Duff. A mid-season variety, the petals being almost flesh-coloured and enhanced by the rich golden anthers of the plant.

President Taft. Which bears huge flowers of flesh-pink.

Souvenir de Louis Bigot. Deep rose-pink attractively flushed with silver.

Vogue. A new peony, bearing flowers of a soft shade of silvery-pink.

Now so rarely seen is *Dictamnus fraxinella*, the Burning Bush of cottage gardens, which grows into a large bush bearing sprays of pleasant purple-pink flowers during June and July. This is a charming plant for the middle of the border and loves a rich, warm sandy soil to make those dense bush-like plants rarely seen in an exposed garden, or in a heavy, cold soil. Like the peony, it is a very long lived plant, increased by cutting the flesh roots into small pieces and replanting in late March, when they will quickly grow away. It is a plant included in my herbaceous border on account of the rich aromatic perfume of both its flowers and of its leaves, rather like that of bergamot, a herb which should be in every garden. Bergamot reached Europe from America about the middle of the sixteenth century and was included in the first book ever written about American plants, that written in 1577 by Dr. Monardes in Seville, after whom the plant was later named, the now familiar *Monarda*. The plant was introduced to England by John Tradescant, about 1620 whilst gardener to the Duke of Buckingham. No plant possesses a more refreshing perfume, it is not so sweet as lavender or rosemary, having some of the aroma of lemons. A few leaves carried in a pocket or handbag on a summer's day will provide a refreshing tonic when inhaled. For pot-pourri, the leaves are dried in late August when they will retain their fragrance throughout winter. It is a plant much used by bees who feed upon its rich crimson and pink flowers.

No plant is of better habit, the flowers being borne on the tops of tiers of bright green foliage. The habit is compact and rarely reaches a height of more than 2 ft. It will also grow well in any soil though it does appreciate some moisture holding peat or leaf mould. Few realise that though bergamot grows well in a sunny border it also grows well in shade and may be planted in the wild garden, the rich crimson varieties being most arresting when used in this way. Late autumn is the best time to plant, the roots being readily propagated by division. *Monarda* is a valuable border plant in that it blooms during late summer and into early autumn, providing the connecting link between the late June magnificence of the border and the chrysanthemums and michaelmas daisies of September. Probably the most outstanding variety is Cambridge Scarlet, which bears a bloom of the richest imaginable crimson-red. A variety bearing a deeper shade is the new Mahogany, whilst Croftway Pink bears a rich clear rose-pink flower. From the *Monardas* was, and in some parts still is, brewed a beverage known as Oswego tea, which possesses a pleasant sage flavour.

Those whose gardens possess a dry wall where catmint has been planted, will be thrilled with its misty mauve flowers produced above its delicate grey-green leaves throughout mid-summer. As an edging to the border, there is no more striking plant especially when it is allowed to overhang a path of crazy paving. But being a lover of dry conditions, it is never lovelier than when planted on a low stone wall, surrounding a lawn or possibly the rose garden with which it blends to perfection.

Like bergamot, catmint (we now call it *nepeta*) was grown for its value in making tea, before the introduction of this drink from the Far East. Catmint tea is still appreciated by those who know it. It took its name from the great fondness of cats for this plant. Not only will they chew it in large amounts, but as the late Frances Bardswell, so rightly points out in *The Herb Garden*, "they roll on it, browse on it and cannot leave it alone". Especially, is this noticeable during very warm weather. An old herbalist once suggested to me after receiving a badly bruised cheek from a cricket ball, that washing the face in the cooled water of boiled fresh catmint leaves would quickly take away the bruise. Whether or not it did so I wouldn't like to say, but try placing a piece of ice in cooled catmint water and splashing it over one's face when returning from a day in the garden, I mean from a day's strawberry picking under a hot, early July Somerset sun, and the catmint will remain with you a firm friend for life.

It is best planted during March, like most blue flowers, *Aster amellus*, delphiniums, and others which never seem quite as hardy as most yellow and white flowers. For winter protection allow the dead foliage to remain until mid-March when new grey growth will be seen growing away from beneath last year's growth. If necessary the plants may then be lifted and divided and replanted into a deeply dug soil.

It is the *Nepeta mussini* that is so well known in our gardens, the species bearing masses of purple-blue flowers. A hybrid, Six Hills Giant, which is taller growing, the blooms being of a deeper purple and which is better planted towards the centre of the border, and the new dwarf *Souvenir d'Andre Chaudron*, which bears light blue flowers are both delightful plants.

Also for edging are several species of the perennial *Verbena*, a plant which is so herb-like in nature that it could well be used to form an interesting edging to a small herb garden. Two species are quite outstanding, possessing that pungent fragrance that is so well known in toilet soap today. One is *V. canadensis*, which bears a succession of flat trusses of deep violet flowers from late June until well into October. The other is *V. corymbosa*, which loves a moist soil and is possibly at its loveliest by the waterside. In habit it is like a hardy heliotrope, being of spreading, almost prostrate habit, the rich violet flowers being borne on wiry stems and they carry much of the scent of the heliotrope. These *Verbena* like a rich soil and nothing is better than some well rotted cow manure and a little peat.

A species quite different from the above forms is the almost shrub-like *V. tridens*, a plant which grows to a height of between 3 and 4 ft. and during late summer literally smothers itself with richly fragrant pale lilac blooms. It is most attractive in either shrubbery or herbaceous border and is greatly loved by bees and butterflies. The *Verbena*, including the annual species, are so valuable in that they provide colour and more especially fragrance right into late autumn.

What a pity it is that lupins possess no perfume, for this in combination with their stately charm and complete hardiness would make them the most outstanding plant in the border. The tree lupin however, *Lupinus arboreus*, a plant which grows into a large bush smothering itself with either white or golden blooms during mid-summer, does carry fragrance and Robinson says "the scent of a single bush reminding one of a field of beans". The two loveliest varieties are Golden Spire and Snow Queen, and they like a dry, warm soil like the catmint. In northern gardens they should be given the overhanging protection of young trees, for if unprotected they may suffer during a severe winter. Nor will the plants grow well in a lime laden soil, which makes it sound as if tree lupins are difficult to grow, when indeed no plant could be easier or more rewarding. It is propagated by sowing seed in April.

Those who enjoy the richly pungent aroma of geranium leaves will love the perennial *Geranium marorhizum*, which bears its clusters of rose-mauve flowers through July and August. The pale green, lobed leaves are very aromatic, especially where the plant is being grown in partial shade. The long, rhizome-like roots are divided in late autumn when it is thought necessary to propagate the plant. If possible plant with it *G. ibericum*, which bears at the same time violet flowers attractively veined with crimson and though the leaves are only faintly aromatic they turn deep crimson in autumn which greatly enhances their value.

One of the most outstanding plants in my border is the common sage, and if a good broad leaved strain can be found, there is no more beautiful plant with its grey-green leaves and indigo-blue flowers often up to 12 inches in length. To obtain the best effect from tall lilies plant them amongst groups of the different sages. In fact one of these days, I hope to make a small border devoted entirely to white border lilies and the various species of sage. It was the red-leaved sage that was so highly esteemed in olden days, and we know that Joseph Cooper, head cook to Charles I would always use the red-leaved variety of the ordinary grey-leaved sage. All the species have aromatic leaves and those of *Salvia argenta*, often 9 inches long and of a pale silver colour are particularly beautiful, but none is more striking than *S. azurea*, which bears spires of bright blue flowers during early autumn. The half-hardy *Salvia patens*, which should be wintered in a frost proof room is particularly handsome with its brilliant sky-blue flowers and neat habit. All the sages are readily increased from cuttings inserted in sandy soil in May.

There is one delphinium species that is fragrant, the interesting *D. Brunonianum*, described in detail with the lilies in Chapter II. If the plant can be obtained it should be in every border, especially one of the pale blue forms which like the blue primrose varies greatly in colouring.

To complete the border of perennial plants, one should plant clumps of sweet-williams and pinks, especially the Allwoodii, which have a much longer flowering season than many of the old cottage border pinks. Though fragrant and seen frequently as an edging to a border, I never feel Mrs. Sinkins pink, or indeed any of the odd varieties, however fragrant, can equal the qualities of catmint or several of the perfumed violas, for after a fortnight's flowering season, the blooms give way to masses of dead, brown heads and the plants though possessing an attractive grey-green foliage, frequently become straggling, the whole plant providing a most untidy look. Use pinks in the border by all means, but not as an edging unless it be one of the free flowering Allwoodii and one with a sturdy, compact habit. In mediaeval days pinks, like the lily-of-the-valley, were used to give additional perfume to wine, for in Parkinson's words, "to strengthen the memory", and it is surprising what value the old gardeners gave to the refreshing of the mind, indeed the scented plant was just as valued as the herb for culinary and medicinal purposes.

CHAPTER VIII

PINKS AND OTHER FRAGRANT DIANTHUS

WE are told that wealthy Romans in the great days of the Roman Empire used various species of Dianthus to flavour wines and foods with the clove perfume we know so well. Through the years the popularity of the dianthus perfume spread across Europe into Germany and France, until it reached our shores with the Norman Invasion, towards the end of the eleventh century. Today in parts of Kent and Sussex the same *Dianthus caryophyllus* which came with the Normans, may occasionally be found growing wild. It was destined to become a parent of the border carnations we now value so much and which in their turn became the parents of the modern Allwoodii. The poet Chaucer wrote of its charms, making special mention of its clove perfume, "the clove gilly-flower," he writes. By late Elizabethan times, the first double carnation had reached us, the old crimson clove-scented carnation which was to bring about a new interest in the plant. Until that time, all dianthus were single and of a pale flesh colour, hence Shakespeare's lines from Henry V.

" 'A could never abide carnation; 'twas a colour he never liked."

The word "pink" is derived from the German Pinksten, which was their name for a small early flowering gillyflower, a name which in Tudor times was used not only to describe all members of the dianthus family, but almost all fragrant flowers including the wallflower and the stock. By the end of sixteenth century, both the pink and the carnation had achieved great popularity and Gerard tells us that a large volume would be needed to describe all the dianthus he knew. In the gardens of the Royal Horticultural Society at Wisley, is to be found the old "nutmeg clove" pink, used in early monastic life to flavour wines. "Of all flowers," wrote William Lawson in his *New Orchard and Garden* published in 1618, "they are the most pleasant to sight and smell." Indeed no garden is complete without the fragrant pink. It is the ideal plant for the small garden hence its popularity today. It is also much sought after by the modern housewife, who is compelled to do her own housework, for it causes her no extra work in dropping its petals, whilst it looks happy in a small vase in even the tiniest of rooms.

On account of their more compact habit, the pink has achieved greater popularity during recent years than the border carnation, for it is also more readily increased by removal of the pipings, as cuttings of pinks pulled from a joint are called, than by layering the shoots. They are also more prolific in producing blooms, whilst the modern Allwoodii will flower over a long period. As a plant for a mixed border it is charming, its rich clove perfume especially noticeable in a walled garden, adding its scent to a host of other perfumes with which it blends to perfection. But rather than use it as an edging plant, try planting a row of pinks behind an edging of catmint, especially lovely are the icy Whiteladies, seen mingling with the misty grey and mauve of the catmint. Apart from their use in the mixed border, pinks are most attractive when planted in small beds entirely to themselves. One of the loveliest displays I ever saw was in an old garden where dwarf box was used to separate the beds each of which took about two dozen plants. Instead of the box, violas could well be used, one variety to each bed and of a variety which possessed a delicate perfume.

RED ALLWOODII	WHITE PINKS	PINK SHADES	LACED PINKS	ALLWOODII SUSAN	SINGLE PINKS

SHINGLE PATH

IMPERIAL PINKS	SHOW PINKS	HERBERTS' PINKS	LACED ALLWOODII	OLD WORLD PINKS	ROCK PINKS

Equally charming a scheme would be to use one of the dwarf lavenders alongside the path and possibly to surround the beds, using catmint to divide each small plot.

A more elaborate pink garden would be to make a small sunken garden, possibly circular in form with crazy paving surrounding and dividing each bed which again may be edged

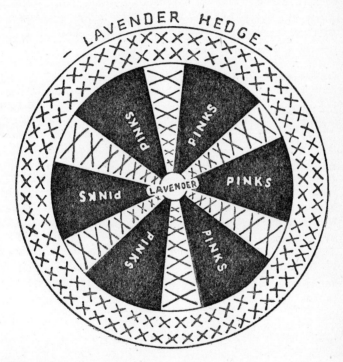

with violas or scented pansies. Space should be made for a garden seat around which orange blossom and buddleias and tall lilies would perfume the air.

There is nothing difficult in the cultivation of pinks except that they are lime lovers and will withstand intense cold but will not tolerate excessive moisture. This was amply proved when growing large numbers of pinks in an exposed garden facing north and more than 1,000 ft. above sea level. Several hundred Allwoodii were planted in September into a soil naturally well enriched with Derbyshire limestone. The winter of 1947-8 was to follow, the severest in living memory when the 300-year-old ash tree groaned under its complete encasing of ice which crunched like a boat in heavy weather tugging at its ropes. Right until Easter were the plants encased in snow and ice, then followed almost six months of continual drought and yet what a superb display these plants gave and at the end of summer each plant must have covered 2 sq. ft. of soil. This was very different from the low lying ground on which I planted pinks in Somerset. They were never happy in the mild humid atmosphere and gradually died away no matter how much attention they were given. No matter then how exposed and cold is one's garden as long as the plants are given plenty of lime and the soil is well drained, pinks will be happy. They like too, an open, sunny position; in no way will they tolerate shade. Manure in quantity they do not like and unless the soil be particularly devoid of humus, in which case some old mushroom bed or well-rotted leaf mould can be given, dig in only lime rubble. Should the soil be light, $\frac{1}{2}$ lb. of lime carbonate per sq. yard should be worked in and this will bind together the particles of soil. For soils of a sticky clay nature, then half the quantity of hydrated lime will break up the soil. They like some potash too, which is best given by way of bonfire ash. Every November when the plants have finished flowering and the beds have been cleaned of weeds, the plants should be given a light dressing of lime rubble and they will require no further attention until the following autumn apart from occasional hoeing.

Pinks and border carnations may be planted either during autumn, but in time for the plants to become settled down before winter, or they may be planted early in spring, it seems to matter little. It is of much greater importance to plant carefully and this means planting not too deeply, only just burying the roots but making them quite firm. Plant 12 inches apart.

Propagation of pinks is almost always either by pipings which are growths pulled out of a leaf joint or socket; and by slips which are side shoots removed with a heel. At any time from mid-May until early October is it possible to remove these growths though June is perhaps the ideal month, for they will root in a compost of peat and sand in less than two months and may be potted into individual pots in autumn. Wintered in a cold frame they will be ready to be planted outdoors at the end of March and will come into flower in early summer. The growth will readily root in a cold frame or even in boxes of sand and peat placed in semi-shade and kept moist throughout the summer.

At the end of summer all plants should be carefully looked over and any straggling growth should be removed, for nothing will spoil a bed of pinks like a plant which has made a lot of weak, straggling growth.

VARIETIES

Almost all the old fashioned pinks possess rich perfume and the list of available varieties has now reached a tremendous size. Many are hundreds of years old and still retain their vigour, whilst others are being added almost daily. First, of the real cottage pinks possessing strong fragrance the following are interesting and charming:

Bridal Veil. An old fringed pink having a full double bloom with crimson centre.

Dusky. Of recent introduction the double dusky-pink blooms are carried on long stems and are of rich clove perfume.

Fimbriata. Fully double creamy-white with fringed petals.

Glory Lyonaise. A glorious variety bearing a double pale pink bloom with a deep cream centre.

Her Majesty. A double white of rich scent, the blooms are borne in great profusion.

Ice Queen. A new white similar in habit to Dusky.

Jane Austen. A charming single pink with fringed petals and coloured mulberry and white.

Ludford Pink. Possessing particularly strong perfume, this is a free flowering variety of cushion habit, the blooms being semi-double and of a rich pink colour.

Mrs. Sinkins. Introduced in 1868 and still a firm commercial favourite. It is of cushion habit and extremely free flowering. It bears creamy-white fringed petals and is double.

Napoleon III. Bears a full bloom of a deep blood-red colour and dates back almost a hundred years.

Old Cottage Pink. The neat lilac-pink blooms are fully double and very strongly scented.

Paddington. A dwarf rose-pink double with crimson eye, grown on the site of Paddington Station.

Sam Barlow. A pink originating in Victorian days and named after the old North Country auricula breeder. It is of rich cream colour with a maroon eye, everybody's favourite.

Sutton Pink. An old pink recently re-discovered in a seaside garden in Lincolnshire. The leaves are of a rich deep green colour, the sweetly scented rose-pink flowers carried on stiff stems.

Waithman's Crimson. Unique in that on each crimson petal are two white marks.

White Ladies. This to my mind is one of the loveliest of all pinks for the pure icy-white flowers are of carnation form and they possess a rich clove perfume.

The laced pinks may be placed in the same category as auriculas in that they were the prized possessions of a few industrial workers of the early nineteenth century and whilst auriculas were being tended and raised by the weavers of Lancashire and Cheshire and the miners of North Derbyshire, the laced pink was an invention of the lace maker's of Paisley and it was the intense friendly rivalry between these raisers that led to so many grand new varieties, many of which have remained with us through the past hundred years or more. But Paisley was not so fortunate as several towns of the North Midlands in being able to retain a countryside on its doorstep and with the rapid expansion of industries along the Clyde, by mid-nineteenth century the cult had almost ceased to exist. But it had created a great national interest in these delightful plants which has endured to this day and with the introduction of several grand new varieties of recent years, including several laced Allwoodii, interest in these plants has never been as high. Indeed there is at present a great demand for laced and picotee edged plants of all descriptions, violas and polyanthus, as well as pinks now increasing in popularity with each year.

The laced pinks all possess a rounded, smooth edged form, almost like small carnations, which gives them a most refined appearance, especially when cut for the home. They have a long life as cut flowers often remaining fresh in water for a fortnight, and what makes them so attractive to the modern housewife, they do not drop their petals.

There are more than a dozen varieties available, several being descended from the old Paisley laced varieties:

Dad's Favourite. Re-discovered by the late Mr. A. J. Macself, growing in a cottage garden in Berwickshire and named thus because the old cottager told of it being grown by his father. Thought to be descended from the Paisley pinks. The blooms are double of purest white, with a dark eye, the petals being laced chocolate colour.

Faith. The first laced Allwoodii. The semi-double flowers are of an attractive old rose colour, laced maroon.

John Ball. Another old variety, the double white blooms being laced with purple whilst the foliage is of an attractive silvery colour.

Laced Conqueror. A lovely pink, the double lilac blooms being laced with pansy-purple.

London Girl. This bears a white ground flower of perfect shape, the petals being laced black.

London Glow. A remarkable variety, the colour being of deepest crimson with a black sheen, the petals having a pure white wire edge.

London Superb. I believe this to be the only laced pink that has fringed petals. The ground is white, the petals deep purple.

Murray's Laced Pink. A very old variety having semi-double white blooms with a wire edging of crimson.

Victorian. Another old fashioned variety, heavily perfumed and possessing huge heavy blooms of pure white, laced black.

The Allwoodii are the result of a cross between the old cottage pink and perpetual flowering carnations. They have a wide colour range, attractive silvery foliage and many of them carry a rich clove perfume. They possess the additional attraction in that they bloom from early summer until the autumn. Some of the most attractive and strongly perfumed varieties are:

Anne. A salmon-pink double with deep salmon eye. Very free flowering.

Bridget. Double flowers of pure shell-pink.

Derek. Rich ruby-crimson, the double flowers being carried on long stems.

Harold. Free flowering double white of lovely form.

Hugh. Rich purple double self.

Julia. Silvery-pink, shaded rose-pink.

Monty. Deep rose-red, with chocolate coloured centre.

Robin. Bright scarlet and orange shades.

Susan. Pale lilac with black centre. Fully double and free flowering, the best of all pinks.

Winston. A strongly fragrant double of a bright crimson colour.

The Show Pinks are the aristocrats of the pink world possessing the free flowering habit of a pink combined with the refined qualities of a carnation. Some of the most exquisite for colouring and perfume are:

Bridesmaid. Introduced by the late Mr. Herbert of Birmingham, the blooms carry a strong perfume and are of a pure shade of shell-pink.

Show Beauty. Of perfect form, the flowers are of a deep shade of rose with a maroon eye.

Show Clove. Very deep pink and strongly scented.

Show Crimson. Of cushion habit, the deep crimson blooms are freely produced.

Show Discovery. A superb pink, the colour being of bright cerise, shaded violet with a black centre. The foliage being of a bright silver shade.

Show Glory. A most striking variety, the colour being of vivid orange-scarlet.

Show Ideal. The bloom is of creamy-white and has an unusual salmon-red ring round the centre.

THE DIANTHUS ON THE ROCKERY

Many species of the dianthus family are ideal for the rockery on account of their clean compact growth. The great trouble with most rockeries is their general untidiness caused by so many plants possessing a straggling habit and the ability of many others to reproduce themselves in vast numbers so that it is difficult to differentiate between weeds and plants and which plants to retain and which to discard. Most members of the dianthus family are of compact habit and each plant may be kept within bounds with the minimum of trouble. Any which tend to become straggly may easily be trimmed with a pair of scissors. It must be said that rock pinks appreciate a liberal quantity of lime rubble and coarse grit incorporated into the soil before planting. Therefore, where a mixed rockery is being planted, preference should be given to lime-loving plants. The flowering period is from early June until early September but care must be given in the choice of plants to cover this extended period.

Most alpine dianthus are ideal for window-boxes, especially for the *Allwoodii alpinus* which flower throughout the summer and grow to a height of only 6 inches. They should be planted into a loamy soil in which has been incorporated lime rubble and coarse sand or grit. Remember that plants in a confined space should never be overwatered. An application of liquid manure water during June and July will help to give added colour to the blooms.

Alpine pinks are ideal subjects for planting on a dry wall as well as on a rockery, but careful consideration should be given to each variety for all have their uses in various ways. Some varieties, which favour a dry sunny position, are ideal for wall tops; those which have almost a trailing habit are most at home in a dry wall. Others, such as the *Allwoodii alpinus* show to advantage between rockery stones, while others should be planted in crevices to afford shelter and shade for their roots. Each and every one have their own characteristics but there will be at least several to be found suitable for every condition.

Many of the rock dianthus are ideal for an edging to a border, path or lawn. The *Allwoodii alpinus* are especially fine and alternate planting of those charming varieties Mars and Wink give a brilliant display of colour. The variety Highland Queen is also excellent for edging.

ALLWOODII ALPINUS

This is a new race of hybrids obtained by crossing the Allwoodii pink with *Dianthus alpinus*. The result is that the plants are ideal for the rockery growing to a height of only 6 inches. The silvery foliage, the compact habit and the beautiful coloured blooms held high above the foliage, makes this a really outstanding introduction. There are several named varieties:

Blossom.   A lovely single mauve with jet black eye.

Dewdrop.   A lovely icy-white with a distinct green eye and possessing a rich clove perfume.

Goblin.   A rich salmon with a dark maroon eye.

Mars.   The best in this section. It is a vivid scarlet double self and very free flowering.

Mercury. Deep cherry-red. The habit is dwarf, but the flowers large and richly fragrant.

Wink. A glistening white having a rich wine-red eye.

Wisp. Pure white with a dark maroon eye.

Now as to species. There are many, but I must be satisfied by giving details of a few of the best:

Dianthus Deltoides. Commonly known as the Maiden Pink, and which grows wild in many parts of Europe and the Near East. The habit is very dwarf and the foliage a vivid deep green which glistens after a shower or heavy dew showing the plant to advantage even during the winter months. The plant is covered with a mass of rich, single pink blooms during June. The value of Deltoides is that it will reproduce itself from seed, by cuttings or even division of the plant in spring. There is also a white variety (albus).

Dianthus Caesius. The old Cheddar Pink whose rich pink blooms are freely produced in June and are most sweetly perfumed. The foliage is a pleasing silvery grey. Unlike most of the dianthus family, the Cheddar Pink will thrive in shade provided the soil is gritty and well drained. The best is Millards' Variety which has a very deep coloured pink bloom.

Dianthus Highland Queen. A hybrid of unusual charm. Growing to a height of 8 inches the single flowers are a rich crimson with darker crimson blotches at the base of the petals. Plants are hardy and flower over a long period.

Dianthus Little Jack. Another hybrid, but perhaps the dwarfest in cultivation growing to a height of only 2-3 inches and having large double flowers of a clear apple-blossom-pink. This variety was raised by Mr. John Gray of Saxmundham and was awarded the R.H.S. Award of Merit in 1930.

Dianthus Multiflorus Salmonea. A really lovely rock variety growing only 6 inches high. The vivid green foliage is shown to advantage by the lovely double salmon-pink blooms.

Dianthus Neglectus. A lovely variety from the Alps. It is perhaps the most valuable of all the rock alpines, on account of its lateness and the great freedom of flowering. It is at its best in August when most of the other rock alpines are getting past their best. The plant must have full sun to allow the vivid cherry coloured blooms to reach perfection. The foliage is compact and has a grass-like appearance and strange as it may seem, the plant will thrive best in lime-free soil.

Dianthus Subacaulis. A native of Spain and the Pyrenees. The blooms grow to a height of only 2 inches and appear to be resting on the foliage which is a vivid rich blue-green. An ideal plant for a dry wall.

Dianthus du Barry. A lovely hybrid having large double blooms of rich lilac. The blooms are borne on 6 inch stems making it an ideal plant for a rockery, for it is extremely showy.

Dianthus Crossways. Another variety so very suitable for a dry wall or for covering rockery stones by planting in a crevice. The cerise blooms have a rich clove perfume and flower over a long period.

Dianthus Caryophyllus. Before leaving the alpine pinks, a word must be said about the oldest form of dianthus we know and from which the modern borders were introduced. It bears a rose coloured single bloom and grows to advantage in rocky crevices where its roots can enjoy shade and the blooms full sun.

Blue Dianthus. This is really a blue perennial sweet-william and is a really outstanding plant. In most gardens it is quite hardy, but not so in a few exposed positions in the north. For this reason it is possibly not more widely grown. In appearance it is very much like the more common sweet-william though the individual blooms are not quite so large, nor is the habit so robust. Growing to a height of 12 inches it is a grand bedding plant with its misty-mauve blooms and grey-green foliage.

Sweet Wivelsfield. Produced by the well-known Allwood Brothers by crossing the sweet-william with the Allwoodii. The result is a very hardy plant of brilliant colouring, in bloom from June until the late autumn. Its compact habit (growing to a height of 12 inches) and great freedom of flowering, makes it one of our most popular bedding plants. For a striking show, the plants should be planted in beds 8 inches apart from seed sown in cold frames in March and transplanted to the open ground in early October. There is both a single and double form, both equally attractive.

Dianthus Loveliness. By crossing Sweet Wivelsfield with *Dianthus speciosus*, Messrs. Allwood Bros. evolved a most unique dianthus in every way. The blooms are more like the enchanting Love-in-a-Mist (*Nigella*) having bearded-like petals of a feathery nature. When planted in a bed to themselves, the effect is most striking, for the plants are covered with a mass of bloom throughout the summer months. Loveliness is easily grown from seed sown in gentle heat or in a cold frame late in March or even in the open in April. It is perennial and very hardy and producing its blooms on 18-inch stems which require little or no staking. Loveliness appears to be set for a great future. Last but not least is its exquisite clove perfume so strong that it will scent a large garden but is at its best early morning or late evening when the dew is on the plants. This superb dianthus may be obtained in a wide range of delicate colours or as a pure white self. Loveliness shows to advantage when massed either in a bed to itself or in clumps at the front of the border.

Many of the new border carnations possess such a sturdy habit that they require no staking in any but the most exposed garden. They are not however as free flowering as the pinks and should be disbudded to obtain the bloom at its best. Again, propagation is by layering the shoots rather than by inserting cuttings which tends to weaken the constitution of the newly rooted plants. Plants may also be grown from seed but cannot be expected to come true to name.

In northern gardens layering should be done in July, but the period may with safety be extended until the third week in August in the south where the rooting period lasts until early October. Too early layering should be avoided as the plants may become lanky during a wet, late summer when they will make too much growth before the autumn frosts arrive to cause them damage. Layering frequently seems to cause the border enthusiast considerable worry, but why I do not know. To anyone with a careful hand, and most gardeners possess this quality, layering is as easy as taking cuttings and infinitely more sure in rooting. Almost all plants will produce a number of shoots which are close enough to the soil for layering and by taking a sharp knife and cutting carefully up to the joint which is nearest to the soil, very many may be layered in a day. The cut should be made up the centre of the stem about an inch in length and should not be taken beyond the joint. Care must be taken not to sever the cutting from the parent plant. The portion of stem which is not connected to the plant is then bent upwards and firmly pressed into the soil. A wire pin bent in the form of a hairpin is placed round that portion connecting cutting to parent and pressed into the soil to prevent the cutting from leaving the ground. Continuing to obtain its nutriment from its parent, the layer will quickly take root, how quick depending upon the degree of moisture in the soil. The time taken is about four weeks under normal conditions compared with twice as long as cuttings severed from the parent. The layer will suffer little from either too wet or too dry conditions though, of course, quickness in rooting depends upon a certain amount of help from the grower. Before any attempt at layering is made, the soil must be quite clear of all weeds and should have had a top dressing of peat and coarse sand in which it is to root. Careful hoeing round each plant before adding the top dressing will do much to retain the moisture content of the soil. Many amateurs place cloches or sheets of glass over their layers. This may be a help during a cold, wet period but is not really necessary for first class rooting results. During the rooting period, little disturbance should be necessary apart from removing an occasional weed and giving a watering should the soil become hard and dry and this is frequently the case during the generally hot month of August. By the middle of the month one or two layers should be carefully lifted to find how the rooting system is progressing and if satisfactory, each should be cut from the parent plant and allowed to remain in position for a few days before putting into 2½-inch pots. This does not cause too great a shock to the young plant.

Perfume in borders has of recent years tended to diminish and it is the rich crimson and whites which may be relied upon to supply our gardens with fragrance. Those I find still carry the genuine old clove scent, and of the others Parkinson said "none will give so gallant a tincture to syrup as the red will do", are:

Crystal Clove.   Bears a bloom of purest white which is sweetly perfumed.

Downs Clove.   A new border of vigorous habit and bearing a bright crimson bloom.

Eglantine Clove.   A strong growing and free flowering salmon-pink with the old clove perfume.

Firetail Clove.   Of a rich buff-apricot shade, overlaid scarlet and exceedingly fragrant.

Kathleen Davis   A white ground fancy, heavily marked crimson.

Leslie Rennison.   Rich lavender, flushed with cerise, the bloom being large and richly fragrant.

Oakfield Clove.   Which bears a bloom of rich glowing crimson.

Old Crimson Clove.   Parkinson's Old Red Clove, so well used for flavouring liquids, and which still carries that tremendous clove perfume.

Robin Thain.   Which bears a pure white bloom striped with scarlet and carries a strong perfume.

Salmon Clove.   A rich salmon coloured carnation, strongly perfumed.

Snow Clove.   A robust grower bearing neat clove-scented flowers.

F

CHAPTER IX

SCENTED-LEAF GERANIUMS

SO interesting are the delightfully fragrant geraniums, possessing so wide a variety of scents and being highly ornamental that they have been given a chapter to themselves, for it is felt that their value in the home or garden is not nearly so appreciated as it would be if these plants were better known.

They are not a plant new to us like the Saintpaulia. They have in fact been grown in the windows of most West Country cottages for about three hundred years for they reached England during the reign of Charles I and at once became popular. They were then used for sweetening the damp, musty rooms of old cottages and manor houses, which for so long had relied on the bowls of delicious pot-pourri to provide indoor sweetness especially during winter when there were few scented flowers in the garden to carry their fragrance through the house. Today, in place of pot-pourri, still used in many of our great houses, we are given synthetic perfumed sprays to keep our homes sweet, but how lovelier it would be to perfume rooms with living plants which the cottagers of the seventeenth century soon came to appreciate. The same delightful plants may be obtained today for the price of a packet of cigarettes, robust and in pots and if tended with care and given a frost-proof room, which almost all our living-rooms are, even in the coldest regions of Britain, the same plants should last almost a lifetime.

Quite happy in partial shade the scented geraniums are particularly suited to the low ceilings of cottages with their thick walls and tiny widows which admit only the minimum of light. It is the leaves of the plant which are fragrant, not the flowers which are quite insignificant, but there are no petals to fall and untidy the room, in fact, the only attention the plants require is occasional watering and even then the plants should be given only water when they really need it. Especially throughout winter should the soil be kept almost quite dry. Then at the beginning of June, when fear of frost has gone, the plants will appreciate repotting and should be allowed to stand outdoors in a sheltered position for a full month or possibly whilst the brilliant summer-flowered pelargoniums or begonias are being enjoyed indoors. Then at the end of August, the plants may be taken indoors and will continue to add their fragrance to the rooms until the following June. The scented geraniums are ideal plants for the town flat or the home with a restricted garden and in this era of small gardens or their complete absence in many of our towns, indoor gardening is the only outlet we have to show our gardening instincts. The plants can remain indoors permanently, or they may be permitted to enjoy the summer sunshine and rains by being placed on a verandah or in a small courtyard. They may be grown in the open in exactly the same way as are the Paul Crampel and Gustav Emich geraniums, used so much for summer bedding but being taller growing they should be given a sheltered situation. The Victorians, who used the scented geraniums wherever possible, would plant them in the protection of a wall or near the house, and also close to a patch where the brushing of the leaves with the long Victorian clothes would create the most delicious fragrance. Especially is their scent noticeable on a still evening after a July shower. If possible, open a window and enjoy their richness for this will never be as pronounced even during their days indoors. Whether to be grown on in the house or in a greenhouse, the plants must be lifted and potted before the frosts arrive. They should then be kept as dry as possible during the winter months.

Recently it was my great pleasure to enjoy the fragrance of these plants to the full in a small Kensington flat, where numerous varieties were placed up the side of the stairs. The ladies of the house brushed the plants with the hem of their skirts whenever they passed up and down the stairs, creating the most pleasing, invigorating perfume which permeated right through the house.

When potting the plants, use if possible, a small quantity of well decayed manure, which sounds quite out of place when describing these fragrant plants, but they really do appreciate a little rotted manure. Or failing this, add some peat to the soil which should be a fibrous loam. The pots too must be well drained by placing broken crocks at the bottom. It is advisable to re-pot at the end of every winter, staking the plants if necessary for several varieties grow tall, and cutting back any side shoots that may have grown too long so as to keep the plant in shape.

Perhaps the most important of all the scented-leaved geraniums is *Pelargonium capitatum*, the essence of which is now used to replace the more expensive attar of roses in perfume. Another possessing the scent of roses is *P. Graveolens*, the variety, Lady Plymouth, having an additional charm in that its leaves are richly variegated.

One of the loveliest of them all is the pyramid-shaped *P. crispum variegatum*, which covers itself in a dense mass of small crimped cream-edged leaves which retain their colour and freshness for years and they are deliciously lemon scented. Besides the enormous range of scents emitted by their leaves, the fact that these scents are pungent rather than sweet is a great point in their favour, for indoors a too sweet perfume tends to become sickly and monotonous, but one never tires of the pungent fragrance of nutmeg, sage, lemons and pepper-mint. Preferably it is better not to mix perfumes indoors unless they be similar. For instance, the lemon-scented *P. crispum variegatum*, is an excellent companion to the *P. crispum minor* which covers itself in small curled leaves, which carry the pungent scent of *Verbena*. But to place either of these plants side by side with the peppermint scented *P. tomentosum*, is to kill much of the fragrance of both. *P. tomentosum*, is unique in that its leaves are thick and velvety and are joined to the main plant by thin long stems giving it a most exotic appear-ance. This is the same plant used by Gertrude Jekyll to make peppermint jelly. She describes the leaves as being "thick as a fairy's blanket . . . and to be found in most old-fashioned gardens". Today we use essence of peppermint and the flavour is not the same. This variety makes a good companion to the eucalyptus scented *P. clorinda*, a variety which will bear during mid-summer a bloom of deep orange-pink shade quite the equal in size and quality to the best of the show pelargoniums. The only other of the scented-leaved varieties to equal this in quality of bloom is Moore's Victory, which bears a rich scarlet flower and whose foliage carries the not too pleasant aroma of pepper.

For pot-pourri, the small leaves of the crispum varieties, there is also *P. crispum major*, which is also richly lemon scented, are the most suitable and retain their perfume for some considerable time. Just remove one or two of the lower leaves so as not to disturb the balance of the plant.

The oak-leaved geraniums carry a rich pungent scent difficult to describe. To some the scent is of incense, to others it is reminiscent of southernwood. It matters little, for the perfume is rich and pleasant, just right for a warm room on a dark winter evening, whilst the leaves are richly coloured and edged with gold. The original oak-leaved varieties and *P. quercifolium* major and minor.

In the same category of geraniums with perfume difficult to define, is the variety *P. fragrans*, which to some is pine scented, to others the leaves smell of nutmeg. An old variety having a definite nutmeg aroma is Lady Mary, listed in the comprehensive catalogue of Messrs. Cannells in 1910 and they suggest that the pungent *P. filicifolium*, with its interesting fern-like foliage is "well adapted for bouquets and button-holes", for which it would be imagined more for its fern-like foliage than for its pungent smell, which would not seem quite suitable for a wedding. But for old churches, which so often smell musty, how valuable would be so many of these fragrant geraniums, placed where their foliage could be brushed by the coats and dresses of those who come to worship. Perhaps the lemon-scented *crispum* varieties would be most suitable, or the sweetly orange-scented, Prince of Orange, which with the minimum of attention will keep fresh and retain its fragrance all the year round. This is an excellent variety for a window box, for it does not grow too tall, likewise the lime-scented *P. nervosum*, which today seems difficult to find in Britain. The slow growing Pretty Polly, whose foliage reminds one of almonds is another very suitable for a summer window-box, for their fragrance will permeate a room especially during a wet day.

For planting in tubs or close to an entrance to a house several varieties will grow to a height of nearly 5 ft. and form dense, well shaped bushes. In favourable parts of Britain, in South Devon and Cornwall, the plants may be left in the open all the year round and may be planted into the open ground. Should the weather be unduly severe such as the winter of 1953-4, the roots may be covered with bracken or straw and sacking. Those living in less fortunate parts would be advised to plant in tubs and to take these to a frost-proof place for the winter and spring and keep the soil quite dry. Possibly the two most outstanding varieties for making specimen plants are Rollisson's Unique, mentioned in Sweet's *Geraniaecae 1820*, which bears strongly mint-scented leaves; and the equally old Scarlet Unique which bears foliage reminding one of incense.

Frequently used for flavouring apple jelly in countries bordering the far shores of the Mediterranean is the apple-scented *P. odoratissimum*, it being so aromatic that but a single leaf is used in the preserving pan.

A variety slightly sage scented is *P. asperum*, which has attractive sharply serrated leaves. For mixing with bowls of summer flowers, sprigs and leaves of many varieties may be used, especially those of the more delicately perfumed varieties such as the almond scented Pretty Polly or Little Gem, and the rose scented *P. capitatum*, and *P. radula rosea*, which makes a dwarf, bushy plant, ideal for the window-box and hanging basket, and bears rich pink flowers. Like *capitatum*, the foliage is also used in the perfumery trade, for it is said to possess the scent of the old cabbage rose.

Two others with unusual perfume are Purple Unique, whose leaves possess the scent of absinthe; and *P. stenopelatum*, the only ivy-leaved geranium with fragrance. It bears bright crimson flowers in summer whilst its leaves carry the aroma of wormwood.

There are others, indeed varieties are being constantly re-discovered growing neglected in the conservatories of old houses which are perhaps to be demolished, or they may be found in cottage gardens hiding their fragrance amidst a wilderness of bygone favourites.

Even a small collection will provide considerable interest,

even if it is confined to the greenhouse where one may spend a
pleasant hour when the sun is setting and the heat of the
summer's day gradually giving way to the cool air of night,
pressing the leaves and trying to find out if the leaves possess
perfumes other than those they are supposed to have. Or has
the day of the garden house gone for ever? There one could
spend those odd hours, generally on Sunday or in the early
hours of an evening, admiring the garden or perhaps the view,
surrounded with scented-leaved geraniums and other fragrant
plants. Or, failing such pleasures, at the end of a tiring day to
carefully remove a leaf from each plant and to take them
indoors and place them in shallow bowls of water and stand
them by the bedside. There throughout the night they will
refresh the air and one is just conscious of them whilst one
slumbers. Those who suffer from sleepless nights would be
advised to place several partially dried leaves of the lemon-
scented varieties in the folds of clean sheets or blankets, for
their fragrance will remain long after the sheets have been put
on the beds. Or place leaves of any of the sweet-smelling
varieties amongst handkerchiefs. Better still, have a few plants
in pots in sitting-room or bedroom, for they will remain fresh
and fragrant for an indefinite time and if cuttings are taken in
August and September, the plants may be quickly increased,
for in a sandy compost they will rapidly root. They should be set
round the edges of a pot in the greenhouse or in a window of the
home and the compost should be kept only just moist. Excess
moisture remaining on the cuttings will cause them to damp off.
In two months they should be rooted and they should then be
removed to small individual pots containing a mixture of loam,
sand and peat where they remain until June. They may then be
planted out for the summer or re-potted into 48 size pots into
a compost containing some rotted manure and within twelve
months of taking the cuttings they will have grown into large,
fragrant plants. But always remember to keep geraniums on
the dry side, not too dry which will cause their leaves to fall,
but if kept too moist they will turn yellow and lose their
perfume.

CHAPTER X

PERFUME IN TULIPS

WHILST hyacinths and many of the sweetly perfumed narcissus are planted for their fragrance quite as much as for their charm, it is not generally realised that the tulip, planted almost entirely for its brilliance of colouring, carries a distinct perfume in a wide range of varieties. Indeed the German, Conrad Gesner, writing in 1559, of the first tulip seen growing in Europe at Augsburg, said ". . . it was like a red lily, with a pleasant smell, soothing and delicate". The important part of his description of this native of Turkey was concerning its fragrance. It was because of their delicate fragrance that the tulip was such a popular flower for evening wear with the ladies of France during the early seventeenth century. But gradually the brilliant colourings of the tulip have ousted our appreciation of its perfume and for so long have the hybridists given us size and colour, that we have almost forgotten to look for perfume in the tulip. It is therefore surprising to find so many choice varieties carrying a distinct perfume. For an early indoor display in pots there is no lovelier variety than the dwarf early single variety, Prince of Austria, with its vivid orange colouring and distinct perfume rather like that of orange blossom. As a companion the richly coloured Yellow Prince, is also pleasantly fragrant; whilst the interesting Crown Imperial, the earliest of all tulips to bloom, which is scarlet edged with gold, carries some of the perfume of a carnation. Another single early with a distinct sweet fragrance is the vermilion Fred Moore. Growing to a height of only 8 inches these dainty tulips are not only so valuable for early pot culture, but equally useful for window boxes or for planting in a rockery or in raised beds.

For pot culture, four or five bulbs should be planted to a small pot or bowl, a pot with drainage holes is better than a bowl with no drainage for fibrous loam and peat can be used and the pots may be allowed to remain outdoors in a plunge bed until late in November which ensures satisfactory root growth. If bowls are used, then prepared bulb fibre must be used for rooting and the bowls placed in a dark cupboard whilst this takes place. But this is so often where one goes wrong with indoor tulips for a cupboard in a warm room is often their home and the heat will bring the bulbs into growth before they have formed their roots. A cool place is essential and where a cellar or barn can be used for rooting, then there should be no trouble.

Single tulips in raised beds and all sections of the tulip should be planted during October as soon as the summer bedding display has ended. Plant the bulbs 3 inches deep and 4 inches apart. Tulips are enhanced if planted with carpeting plants and several of the early flowering primrose hybrids possess a delicate fragrance. A choice of one of these may be made from those mentioned in the chapter on spring flowers. Double tulips, bearing a very fully petalled bloom do not require carpeting plants.

The double earlies offer a wider selection of scented varieties. Like the early singles they may be grown indoors or in the open and require similar treatment. The white and rose shaded Murillo and its many "sports" are all fragrant, but my own favourite is the honey-scented Tearose, which bears a soft yellow bloom, flushed with salmon-pink. Especially is its perfume noticeable on a still May evening, and in a walled garden which seems to gather evening fragrance about itself. The pure white, Schoonoord, is also honey scented and outstanding when planted with one of the scarlet or crimson varieties, which unfortunately do not seem to possess perfume to any marked degree.

Richly fragrant too is the double of more recent introduction, the rich crimson, edged gold Marquette, of excellent sturdy habit and ideal for an exposed garden. Only recently did I discover that it is a "sport" of the old Murillo, which accounts for its rich perfume.

Several of the Breeder tulips now so popular, both for bedding and cutting, for which their sturdy stems and purple and bronze colourings make them particularly suited, possess perfume. None is lovelier than the large flowered golden-bronze, flushed purple, Cherbourg, a new variety, which appreciates the protection of a wall as it is rather tall growing. Where possible, plant the bulbs near a window where their rich lily-of-the-valley fragrance will permeate right through the home during May and early June.

In Darwin's only a very few seem to possess a distinct fragrance and two are of more recent introduction. Can it be that perfume in tulips is now engaging the attentions of the hybridists? The lovely deep violet-blue Demeter, is quite strongly scented of clove pinks, whilst the deep yellow Golden Age, has a pleasant sherry perfume. The new variety White Victory, is said to carry the fragrance of jasmine.

Tulips with violet-blue colouring do seem to possess more fragrance than others for of the older Darwins, the reddish-violet Cordelia and the purple-maroon Philippe de Commines, both still superb varieties, carry strong fragrance. Another, Nauticus, deep rose coloured, shaded violet, also carries a slight but distinct fragrance.

The only Parrot tulip to possess a distinct perfume is the novelty Black Parrot, a recent introduction, which in addition to its interesting black-fringed petals, carries a rich fragrance. It is a "sport" of Philippe de Commines, which explains its perfume.

Of the cottage tulips, so valuable in that they may be obtained in a much wider range of lovely yellow colourings than any other section, the deep yellow Mrs. Moon carries a distinct almond perfume and its attractiveness is more enhanced by its long pointed petals. The new lily-flowered Marietta, deep satin-rose which is a grand bedding variety for an exposed district, growing to a height of only 16-18 inches, is attractively fragrant; but what has become of that lovely variety Primrose Beauty, so well named for it possessed the true soft primrose colouring and also its perfume? It was the only tulip that carried the true perfume of the woodlands which it retained even when cut.

Where possible plant these taller growing and sweetly perfumed tulips beneath a row of lilacs which are in bloom at the same time during late May and early June. Of the Darwins, the maroon Philippe de Commines looks most handsome planted beneath the new lilac, Primrose; or under a lilac hedge of one of the lovely pure white varieties. In the same way the almond scented Mrs. Moon appears very attractive planted beneath purple lilacs, especially with the double reddish-purple and very fragrant Charles Joly.

Tulip beds too, look only at their best if edged with a low box hedge or a thick row of a dwarf late spring-flowering plant, such as the richly perfumed double French primrose, Marie Crousse, which covers itself with large deep mauve blooms. And interplant the beds in October with wallflowers, using the pale yellow, Primrose Dame, with one of the purple tulips. Then complete the bed with an edging of primrose Marie Crousse and you will be rewarded with almost an over-powering fragrance on any sunny day in late spring. Against a white-washed wall of a cottage such a display will be shown off to the full and in addition one will be able to inhale the delicious perfume.

Of the tulip species, which should be more widely known, several possess distinct fragrance, none being richer than *T. persica*, a species which grows to a height of only 4-5 inches and if left alone on the rockery will seed itself abundantly. It bears its orange and bronze blooms, several on a stem, during early June and is the last of the tulips to bloom. *T. sylvestris*, also carries a rich perfume. It is the species found wild in meadows in certain parts of England and in Europe, bearing its yellow, star-like blooms on 12-inch stems. It should be planted in partial shade and in a part of the garden where it may be left undisturbed for years. Similar is *T. australis*, though it is not quite so tall and the blooms are shaded with crimson.

Not only should the lovely *T. sylvestris*, be planted in grass and the partial shade of trees, but try a massing of the taller growing and fragrant tulips in the grass of the orchard or bank, or in the woodland garden. Plant them with some of the sweetly scented jonquils and narcissi and you will be agreeably surprised at their charm. Far too long has the tulip been used only for formal bedding and so much of its charm is missed in this way. Try planting the violet-blue Demeter together with the pale yellow Mrs. Moon down the sides of a path or drive backed with the glaucous green foliage of cupressus trees. No matter if the grass is long and neglected, the display will be one of great charm. And to keep the garden work at a minimum, leave down the bulbs, merely cutting off the seed heads when the blooms have faded and the petals have fallen.

CHAPTER XI

BULBS WITH PERFUME

WHEN scented bulbs are mentioned it requires little thought to think of the hyacinth and certain narcissi and the jonquil and there one must stop to think. There are, however, numerous species not nearly so frequently grown as they should be which are easy, inexpensive and delightful when planted in pots for indoor cultivation, or in various parts of the garden.

The lovely milk-white flowering snowdrop, the first of the bulbs to bloom, is known to all gardeners. Even the smallest of gardens will have clusters of them grouped round the trunks of trees or planted as an edging to a path. But few realise that many of the snowdrops possessed distinct perfume which they now seem to have lost. *Galanthus plicatus* in particular, was highly fragrant, but these natives of Eastern Europe seemed to have lost their perfume when they reached our shores.

A recent hybrid of *Galanthus nivalis*, the common snowdrop introduced from Germany about a century ago, called Arnott's Seedling, possesses a rich perfume. The large blooms are borne on stems almost a foot in length, the blooms being of immense size with the outer perianth petals almost an inch long, the inner petals being attractively marked with bright green crescents. This will become a most popular cut flower when it becomes better known for it blooms during February and like the common snowdrop multiplies rapidly when established. It should be planted in a sheltered corner, where winter winds will not cut it down for it is rather tall growing for winter flowering. The plant received an Award of Merit from the Royal Horticultural Society in 1951. Plant in grass and around the clusters plant the common single and double snowdrop to lend it some protection and to conceal some of its long stem.

It is not generally realised, that the Muscari, the grape hyacinths, are almost all richly fragrant. Several of the species carry a distinct almond blossom perfume particularly *M. comosum*, the tassel hyacinth, which bears its vivid purple and green blooms on 12-inch stems and is excellent for cutting in April. *Muscari Tubergenianum*, which received an Award of Merit from the Royal Horticultural Society in 1950, and which bears rich turquoise blooms in great profusion is also sweetly scented, whilst *M. moschatum flavum*, the musk hyacinth, should be in every room of the home. Planted in pans or small pots, it bears its sedate purple and yellow blooms early in March, their tremendous perfume permeating right through the house. The blooms are not particularly attractive, but for indoor flowering and for a sheltered corner near the house, a few bulbs of this Muscari should be included in every bulb order.

Grape hyacinths look most attractive when planted with daffodils, especially with the large trumpet flowered King Alfred, of deep uniform gold; or with the pure icy-white Mount Hood. Or with the sweetly perfumed jonquils they look most attractive and clustered about the rockery with several of the dainty miniature daffodils which possess considerable perfume too.

Several of the dwarf bulbous iris possess a delicate scent, none being more attractive than *Iris Reticulata*, the "netted" iris so called because of the net-like covering of its bulbs. Outdoors it sends up its sturdy looking blooms whilst the snow still covers the ground. All it needs is a position such as beneath a wall, where it may catch a glimpse of the winter sun. The bulbs should be planted in September into a soil containing some lime rubble and they may be left down for years. They make delightful pot plants for indoor flowering for they will come into bloom in January in a cool room. They will in no way tolerate forcing conditions. Again, they are happiest in a soil containing some lime rubble and a little peat. Several pots placed in a window where the sun's rays will occassionally penetrate will show their lovely velvety purple blooms to advantage. The bright orange splash on the fall petals adds to their mid-winter brightness. The variety J. S. Dijt, almost crimson in the winter sun is also deliciously fragrant; whilst the new introduction, Cantab, bears blooms of brilliant

Cambridge blue, which stand up to the most severe of winter gales, and give off their perfume during the dullest of weather.

Those who have a barren corner in the garden, whether in town or country, should plant it with the sky-blue flowered, *Iris stylosa*, which when comfortably settled down will bear its richly perfumed flowers throughout the bleakest winter. But it must be given a soil entirely devoid of all humus and manure, though it thrives on lime rubble which should be added in quantity. *Iris histrioides* too, possess a distinct perfume, rather like violets and like those mentioned it also blooms during mid-winter though it likes an hour of sunshine to open its flowers of brightest steel-blue. It is happiest on a rockery, facing the sun and where it can remain undisturbed for years. These lovely irises should be planted amongst drifts of winter flowering crocuses for a most satisfying display during the darkest winter day.

No garden of fragrance is complete without the crocus which possesses the scent of warm honey only when the blooms are warmed by the early spring sunshine though *Crocus longiflorus*, carrying the fragrance of wild roses, begins to open its long lavender tubers early in December, and *C. vernus* and *C. versicolour*, take over towards the end of January. The latter variety possesses only a faint perfume, but the corms are so inexpensive and free flowering that it is surprising it is so neglected. *C. vernus*, a native of Southern Italy was cultivated by the Romans for its rich perfume, the petals being dried and used for filling cushions and couches, whilst the Roman women bathed in water fragrant with the scent of the flowers. Most attractive for planting amongst the winter flowering irises are *C. vernum alba*, almost as white as snow, and the new hybrid Vanguard, which is bright blue.

The fragrance and beauty of the bluebell is so common to all flower lovers that only when we have been abroad and return to Britain in May do we appreciate the native bluebell, *Scilla nutans*. Nowhere does it look more charming, nor is its fragrance more powerful than when seen in the woodland garden, planted in long grass in the dappled shade of deciduous trees. The loveliest sight of the native bluebell I ever had the pleasure to see was the dense, rippling mass of purple-blue of the old tilting green of Biddulph Castle, my old home. The "sea" of bluebells was backed by an avenue of stately lime trees which shut out the sky with their pale green leaves each May. The perfume of the flowers could be inhaled almost a mile away. But where planting *Scilla nutans* in an orchard, where they look charming beneath pink May apple-blossom, do not overlook the fragrant white variety and the rose-pink scillas equally as lovely if not quite so scented.

For later flowering *Scilla amethystina*, which bears large spikes of clear blue flowers in June, is also very fragrant. The blooms are carried on only small stems so it should be planted in the rockery or around the roots of apple trees. Also suitable for planting in a rockery or in short grass is the rich blue *S. pratensis*.

The first of all the scillas to bloom are the Siberian scillas, which bloom in March and April and which make a brilliant show in a shrubbery, planted in tufts. They are lovely too in the rockery or planted beneath tall trees which cover the ground with their withered leaves. The white variety *S. alba*, should be planted with the vivid electric-blue of the true Siberian bluebell.

Scilla italica is yet another possessing rich perfume. It is hardy and like all other scillas thrives best in a warm, sandy soil. Its intense sky-blue flowers are borne on 9-inch stems making it most suitable for cutting for the home.

Where possible, plant them against the richly coloured bark of silver birch trees, the silver and blue effect being outstandingly beautiful.

Whereas so many bulbs which possess rich perfume are neglected, especially for flowering indoors, the hyacinth has always reigned supreme as a fragrant spring flower for the house if not now so popular for garden planting owing to its too stiff habit. For centuries the plant has been cultivated in Britain, the Elizabethan gardener Gerard knew it and Parkinson in his *Paradisus* writes, "The common Oriental hyacinth, I call it common because it is now so plentiful in all gardens that it is almost not esteemed. . . ." It is surprising that Parkinson makes no mention of its perfume. The double hyacinth is said to have been introduced to our shores from

Holland by a Peter Voerhelm in 1720, which was the variety which he named King of Great Britain, the bulbs costing as much as £200 each. The late Miss Eleanour Sinclair Rohde, tells us that as late as the mid-nineteenth century, double flowered hyacinth bulbs often made as much as £10 each and today owing to the prolonged time it takes to bring a bulb to maturity, they are priced higher than all other bulbs. But a single bulb in a small pot will fill a large room with its perfume. Of their rich sweetness may be quoted Francis Bacon of the breath of flowers being far sweeter in the air than in the hand. Which is so very true of the hyacinth indoors, too many growing together in a small room making the atmosphere almost sickly sweet as does orange blossom for a few hours.

Hyacinths indoors like a moisture holding compost; remember how well the hyacinths used to flower when as youngsters we would grow them in a jam jar containing only water? Use a fibrous loam containing some peat and some well rotted manure and plant the bulbs with the nose just above soil level.

Outdoors a similar compost should be used. *The Flower Garden* written by McIntosh, gardener to H.M. The King of the Belgians and published in 1838, gives the preparation of the soil for hyacinths in considerable detail saying that the compost used by the celebrated Dutch growers of Haarlem, consisted of "leaf mould, fine sand and well rotted cow dung". Interestingly he goes on to say that the leaf mould should consist of the "leaves of elm, birch and lime; those of oak, beech, walnut, chestnut and plane being too long in rotting". And yet I always thought the leaves of oak and beech made the best leaf mould. Today we would use peat in any case.

Using cow manure, sand, loam and leaves, the Dutch growers made up a compost which was of such richness that it would "retain its virtues for seven years". Gardeners of today who sprinkle a packet of artificial fertiliser about the soil and expect equally outstanding results, would do well to remember that in gardening there is no quick way to success, the land gives back only what is put into it both in labour and in compost.

All the old writers on hyacinths stress the need for deep

G

planting, 6 inches at least, with the bulbs resting on a small mound of sand, which still seems to be the best method of planting.

It is said that many of the old Dutch growers catalogue nearly a thousand different varieties and there is still a very wide colour range today. None is lovelier than the rich yellow City of Haarlem, which possesses a delicate perfume making it most suitable for room culture. In beds outdoors this variety looks most attractive planted with the pale blue Bismarck. Or plant the new japonica red, Cycloop, or the almost crimson, Jan Bos, with the deep lavender-blue-flowered, Grand Maitre.

For Christmas flowering indoors the less formal Roman hyacinths in blue, pink and white are most attractive. They should be planted in August four or five bulbs to a bowl, for the bulbs are smaller than the oriental hyacinths and brought on in gentle heat as soon as they are well rooted. A new hybrid hyacinth called Rosalie, can also be brought into bloom for Christmas, its bloom being of a pleasing shade of warm pink. The new multiflora hyacinths, each bulb bearing up to eight flower spikes are more than attractive for pot or outdoor culture, and may be obtained in pure white, rose-pink and pale blue shades.

It is only the large trumpet narcissi that are rightly called daffodils, and they possess no perfume. The rest are classed as narcissi and a number, especially the pheasant eye and bunch-flowered varieties possess a distinct and rich fragrance. It is only in the orchard or woodland garden or planted informally alongside a cottage path that the narcissus is happiest. Planted in beds, in long straight rows, it looks quite out of place, though the formality may be relieved by inter-planting with the rich purple Juliae primrose Fruhlingzauber, or with purple aubretia.

Parkinson devotes some forty pages of foolscap size to describing the many forms of narcissus and daffodil known to early Stuart gardeners. Of the many he describes as possessing perfume, none is more interesting than his description of the green autumn flowering daffodil which "smelleth very sweet" and which "sheweth not the flower until October". Would that this lovely flower be known to us today, but many of the interesting species he mentions may still be found, so delightful are they, reminding one of the true woodland daffodil which always seemed to possess the true woodland fragrance, a mixture of pine and wild roses, primroses and oxlip.

Deliciously fragrant are the Campernelles, *N. odorus*, which bear their clusters of bright yellow flowers on 9-inch stems during April. They should be planted freely about the shrubbery or amongst the orchard trees so that they may be cut in quantity for the house and mixed with other less fragrant narcissi.

Closely related to them are the Jonquils, also natives of Spain and North Africa. The double form known as Queen Anne's Jonquil, is perhaps the most fragrant of all flowers. Plant them where possible where they may receive some spring sunshine for they like best the dry conditions of their native land.

Enchanting subjects for the rock garden and the alpine house where they will come into bloom early in spring are the angel's tears daffodils, *N. triandrus albus*, known in Ireland as Gannymedes Cup. The dainty globular flowers are suspended on 6-inch stems giving the effect of tear drops and which carry a pleasantly delicate perfume. They look most charming planted in small earthenware pots, the soil covered with shingle, white if possible. Outdoors, plant them in a soil almost devoid of manure or humus. They are unlike most other daffodils in that they thrive best in a dry, almost parched sandy soil. In a soil which retains moisture the bulbs seem to rot away during a wet winter.

Another possessing rich perfume is *N. Canalicatus*, which is like a tiny polyanthus narcissus, its small white blooms having rich golden cups. The last of all to flower is *N. gracilis*, so strongly fragrant and which bears its sulphur-coloured blooms right into June.

Of the large flowered narcissi grown in vast quantities for garden display and for cutting, the late flowering Double White possesses a rich perfume, so do most of the Tazetta or bunch-flowered section, particularly the early flowering Cragford, which bears up to six blooms on a stem, the perianth being purest white, the cup vivid orange-scarlet. Similar, but later flowering is the variety Geranium and Scarlet Gem, with its yellow perianth and golden-yellow cup. All are delightful when massed down the sides of a path or beneath small trees, so too are the large flowered Jonquil hybrids, particularly rich in perfume being the bright yellow Golden Sceptre and the moonlight yellow, Trevithian, both of which look most attractive and smell so sweet in the late evening.

The old Pheasant's Eye narcissus, *N. recurvus*, which was so well named and which is very late in flowering, is strongly fragrant and should be planted beneath a wall in soil enriched with manure and decayed leaves, where it may be left down for years to produce masses of its scented blooms for cutting in May.

Before leaving this chapter on bulbs, may I make a suggestion for bulb lovers which I am sure would give weeks of pleasure and that is to plant a bulb border backed by a wall or wattle hurdles to shelter the plants from strong winds. Plant the bulbs in clumps of half a dozen, placing at the back the taller growing tulips with fragrance and at the front the strongly scented musk grape-hyacinth and the miniature narcissus. Plant them so that there will be an interesting display right from the early New Year until mid-summer, six months of charm and fragrance with something for taking indoors every day. If you like, fill up any spaces with wall-flowers or scented primroses, Marie Crousse, or the winter-flowering Barrowby Gem, and make an edging of scented violets to keep the border tidy. Do not fill the border with herbaceous plants or shrubs which will prevent the thorough cleaning of the border in autumn and which will rob the bulbs of moisture, sunshine and food. Each autumn the border can be cleaned, mulched with peat or some rotted manure and more wallflowers can then be planted. By all means cover the hurdles or wall with winter jasmine or fragrant honeysuckle, but leave the scented shrubs to themselves. To provide late summer and autumn colour plant the summer snowflakes, *Leucojum aestivum* and the true autumn crocus. They carry little perfume but are delightful in themselves and will keep the border colourful until the year end. Several of the fragrant lilies too, *L. Regale, Henryi* and *Hansoni*, all inexpensive, will add fragrance and colour through late summer and early autumn.

Nor must we forget the sweetly-scented *Cyclamen Europaeum*, which blooms in sun or shade through late summer and into autumn, its dainty blooms hovering above the marbled foliage like dozens of crimson butterflies.

Then there is the sweetly-scented freesia, until recently a greenhouse flower, but now with the introduction of a new hardy strain the bulbs will flower in the open in a normal summer. They should be given the protection of heather or some other dwarf-growing shrub. Several of the thymes are ideal and will afford some protection from excess moisture and will also support the thin grass-like foliage and rather frail stems. Freesias, being lovers of dry, sunny conditions will look most attractive planted amongst the thymes on a sunny, dry bank or in a sunny bed containing plenty of sand. The bulbs are planted in early April and it is essential that until they have rooted and the grassy foliage can be seen above the soil, some protection be given. Normally the foliage of heather or thyme will give the necessary protection, but should the weather be unduly wet, bracken or long straw placed over the covering plants and removed as soon as conditions permit, will provide the necessary protection. There is a wide range of glorious varieties, all fragrant, but with the pink and yellow coloured hybrids particularly so.

There are others, but this will be sufficient to make a start to forming a collection of fragrant bulbs.

CHAPTER XII

THE HERB GARDEN

BECAUSE we can so easily purchase a packet of herbs even if only sage and thyme from the grocer, herb gardening in Britain seems to be one art of horticulture which has, alas, now almost disappeared. In any case, few herbs are now used either medicinally, or culinary, we prefer cabbage boiled long hours in water and we have lost the art of enjoying good food whilst our digestion suffers as a result. I remember so well my grandfather's herb garden, a veritable blaze of colour throughout summer with sage in all its purple glory; the red and pink and white valerian; the crimson bergamot and the golden heads of tansy. Mixed with the green foliage of such diverse colouring, the grey leaves of sage, the shining apple-green of mint, the deep almost cupressus green of the various thymes, all combine to give the herb garden a richness of colouring not found elsewhere in the garden. Then in addition, is the pungent scent of the various plants which provide hours of interest and enjoyment, collecting and pressing the various leaves in much the same way as we did when children, the scented leaves of the geraniums. And what a lot is missed in drying the herbs and taking them indoors for pot-pourri, or for making up into muslin bags, quite apart from their great value in the kitchen.

Perennial herbs are almost indestructible too, bushes of rosemary and lavender and bay will last for centuries, remaining evergreen through winter. "For December and January," said Francis Bacon, "you must take such things as are green all winter, bays, rosemary, lavender, juniper." The herb garden is therefore always a point of interest all the year round, unlike the herbaceous border, which remains quite uninteresting when once the michaelmas daisies are over in early November and until the fresh green of the delphiniums peeps above the soil in early May.

The herb garden was attached to every home in Saxon times and continued right down to the beginning of the present century. It was generally set out into small beds divided by small paths of gravel, or hedges of box and each bed contained just one variety of herb. It was almost always surrounded by a wall or by tall hurdles and given a position where the sun will reach, not the damp, shaded corner which the modern gardener uses to grow a root of mint and possibly a single plant of sage. To mediaeval and Tudor gardeners herbs were of the utmost value not only in cooking and for medicinal purposes, but many varieties were used to cover the floors of dwelling houses and places of worship, the earth floors becoming sour and evil smelling without the fragrance of the herbs. And so, the herb garden was of vital importance and was cultivated with the reverence in which the plants were held. Several flowering plants known to us today for their charm rather than for their culinary or healing value were also included in the herb garden, chiefly the rose, the lily, the violet and the primrose, but all possessed perfume for sweetening foods and for purifying the air of buildings. Meats were generally cooked in the waters distilled from various herbs, marjoram and rose water being the most popular and there being no sugar, violet water was used quite as much as honey for flavouring drinking water so often sour.

In mediaeval days herbs were grown in vast quantity by the monasteries, for the monks then acted as doctors for miles around their foundation. The herbs were always dried in special drying rooms, hence the modern word "drug" from the Anglo-Saxon "drigan", meaning "to dry". The great age of our herbs which have been classed as "garden" herbs is revealed in a chapter in a manuscript written by the Abbot of Cirencester, *De Naturis Rerum*, at the end of the twelfth century. In it will be found the first writings on horticulture which tells us that "The garden should be adorned with roses and lilies, heliotrope, violets and mandrake. There you should have parsley, fennel, southernwood, sage, rue, lettuce, cress and peonies." Every plant, be it noted, possessed rich fragrance in addition to culinary properties.

Four hundred years later Parkinson tells us that "Rue is a

strong herb and helps much against windy bodies", indigestion being a troublesome complaint even in Stuart times. Valesian he tells us "is used to provoke sweating, to expell evil vapours that might annoy the heart", and Solomons seal, then freely planted for its medicinal properties, was said to be an excellent herb "to consolidate and bind", meaning the flow of blood of a wound. Featherfew, Parkinson tells us, "is a herb of greater use for women than for men, to dissolve flatulence which causeth the pains of the mother". Though many of the cures suggested by Parkinson would not be given serious consideration by the medical pofession today, several herbs are still suggested by them. Is there a better cure for blood pressure than nettle tea?

Equally delightful would the herb garden be today. Chopped herbs of almost every variety we know of adds interest and spice to a diet which we in England have come to accept, left-overs from war days. No salad is complete without its chopped chives and mint and a host of other tasty plants, modern beef is almost uneatable without large helpings of horseradish cream, the flavour of certain fish is enhanced with leaves of bay or chopped sage and thyme and parsley. For those who find the modern diet so dull, may I make the suggestion that a dish of herbs should be on the table for every meal, for even if you don't partake, their fragrance is most satisfying during meal times. Today we are a nation of sandwich eaters and how much more appetising they become when their contents are sprinkled with chopped herbs. Try something different each time, sage or thyme with cheese, as an example.

Again, the value of herbs for their indoor fragrance is not nearly so much appreciated as it should be. Those who find sleep difficult in coming should try filling small muslin bags with the dried leaves of eau-de-Cologne mint with those of rosemary or bergamot. Hang them about the bedroom and their fragrance will soon bring about sleep.

The use of those large bowls of pot-pourri is now so rarely seen. How pleasant they are in the rooms of that most charming of country houses, Burton Agnes Hall in Yorkshire, where they diffuse a different fragrance in almost every room.

Scents for the mind played an important part in early days, particularly during the latter Tudor and early Stuart period. "The true thyme is a special help to melancholy", the old gardeners tell us and add "is also much used for the toothache." For a headache there is no better cure than inhaling the dried leaves of lemon thyme from a muslin bag. Lavender we are told was used to perfume linen and apparel, and the dried flowers "to comfort and dry up the moisture of a cold brain". Today, its use is similar for quite apart from its use for perfume, the dried flowers mixed with peppermint are a great help to combat the ordinary head cold.

Of rosemary, Gerard, the Elizabethan writer on horticulture, says "if a garland there of be put about the head, it comforteth the brain . . . and the heart and maketh it merry." It was frequently used at funerals, given to friends to inhale as a comfort. With lavender, marjoram and southernwood, which as children we always knew as "lad's-love", rosemary forms the basis of the herbs used in pot-pourris with the petals of roses, clove-scented pinks and honeysuckle.

Useful in so many ways, almost indispensable to the herb enthusiast but so sadly neglected are the herbs, even a small herb garden planted at the bottom of a garden path where the plants are easily reached, for gathering the foliage several times a day will prove of untold value, interest and fragrance. But here let it be said that for their leaves to fully mature and carry a richness of flavour and perfume they must be grown in a sunny position and in a rich, well-drained soil. They like too, an open airy situation where Frances Bardswell tells us "they drink it (air) in with joy, and breathe it out again in fragrance". So frequently do we see an odd plant struggling beneath a shady tree or planted near the rubbish heap where it receives only the minimum of sunlight and air. Herbs build up in their leaves and stems natural oils which remain vigorous and active for a long period, but only do these oils form when the plant is exposed to the maximum of sunlight. It must be remembered too that most herbs are natives of the hot, dry Mediterranean area, where they contain a richness of perfume little known to English grown herbs unless the summer be particularly warm and sunny. To plant herbs in a sunless corner just because they are herbs is not only to deprive them of the full richness of their properties but the charm of the well-planted herb garden can never be realised. Having selected a suitable position, the soil should then be prepared and a note made of the cultural requirements of the individual plants.

Alecost. Sometimes called Costmary, this is a herb which few seem to realise exists at all. It is perennial and will be too strong growing for the small herb "patch", but its leaves are so useful to put in stews and soups. The leaves are long with serrated edges and then smell like mint. Frances Bardswell says "like weak mint-sauce" which may be more accurate. It is a useful herb in that its white flowers may also be used for their fragrance when dried.

Balm. For the fragrance of its foliage in the garden this plant rivals lavender, southernwood and rosemary, indeed even where no herbs are being grown several plants of each should be grown in the shrub border entirely for their outdoor perfume I well remember the appetising balm "tea" made by my grandmother from its fresh green leaves which was so good for the 'flu. But whether it is used in this way or not the fragrance of its leaves, especially when crushed and when moist is a special delight in the garden. Its scent is that of rich verbena; George Whitehead in *Garden Herbs* suggests that it emits "the sweetest odour of all herbs". A bush is best confined to the shrubbery for it grows bushy and tall and needs plenty of room. It likes a sandy loam and a place in the sun. There is an attractive variegated golden leaved variety, excellent for the shrub border but its fragrance is not so pronounced.

Bay. Most of us know the shiny-leaved bay trees, rather like the Portugal laurel, which are now so popular as specimen tub trees for the entrances to houses. This is a delightful way to use them, but it should be remembered that in exposed gardens where they receive frost and winds during winter their foliage should be covered with clean sacking, or the tubs should be removed to a sheltered position. For tub planting use a good loamy soil containing a little well-rotted manure and do not allow the roots to suffer from too dry conditions. The leaves, so pleasant in milk puddings or even one allowed to stand in a glass of milk for half an hour before drinking, should be removed from the tree just prior to using.

Bergamot. See Chapter III. (*Monarda*).

Catmint. See Chapter III. (*Nepeta*).

Cotton Lavender. Also known as French lavender, was one of the herbs grown in ancient days for covering the floors of churches and houses, for its carries a strong refreshing perfume whilst the foliage remains green or grey (depending on the variety) all the year round. It makes an ideal small hedge and is often found in the old established herb gardens grown in this way for dividing the plots. Its botanical name is *Santolina*, there being a grey and a green leaved species both of which have dainty pale yellow flowers.

Hyssop. This is a lovely herb which bears dark green leaves and bright blue flowers during August and September. There is also a small leaved species very suitable for planting on a rockery and also a species which bears attractive pale pink flowers. The leaves are evergreen, the plant very suitable for the front of a shrub border as it reaches a height of about 20 inches. The leaves are fragrant and are mentioned as being used at the sprinkling of the altars at the consecration of Westminster Cathedral. "The whole plant is of a strong sweet smell", so Parkinson tell us and goes on to state that it is "a special remedy against the sting of an adder".

Like balm it likes a light, sandy soil and plenty of sunshine. It is propagated by pulling rooted pieces of the hardwood away from the base in April. Besides its fragrance in garden and home its fresh leaves are used in soups and salads.

Lavender. Found in English gardens since Roman times and known to all garden lovers. It grows in any well cultivated soil but prefers chalkland which seems to bring out its fragrance to a marked degree. It is propagated by removing cuttings with a heel during late summer. If inserted in a frame containing pure sand to which has been added a little peat, rooting will take place over winter and the young plants may be planted out in May. The flower spikes should be cut for drying during August, the varieties for providing the most amount of bloom are the Old English and the Seal variety, both of which are valuable when grown as a hedge. They are the two best lavenders for oil distillation and grown commercially for this purpose. The flowers should be removed just before they are fully dried in order for them to retain their maximum perfume.

Another variety suitable for a hedge is Grappenhall, whose flowers are deep purple. The pure white, *alba*, planted with Grappenhall, makes a most attractive contrast. Its blooms are deliciously scented like most white flowers and though scarce is quite hardy as well as being a vigorous grower.

The dwarf varieties, suitable for the herb garden or for an attractive edging to a rose garden are the silvery leaved Dutch variety; the dark flowered Munstead; Loddon Pink with its charming and unusual pale pink spikes; and the Hidcote lavenders which also possess pronounced silvery foliage and are the most dwarf and slowest growing of all lavenders. Another of dwarf habit and which is the first to flower is Wilderness lavender, which bears unusually dark green leaves. The nearest to a blue-flowered lavender is Folgate Blue, which is also dwarf of habit.

The flower spikes are removed in August before they become dried on the plant for they retain their fragrance, provided by the natural oils of the plant, better if dried off the plant in an airy room rather than by the direct rays of the sun. Do not discard the stems of lavender which if slowly dried and allowed to remain unbroken may be burnt in the same way as incense filling a room with rich lavender perfume.

Marjoram. Sweet marjoram it was called in olden days and is highly aromatic both in the garden and when used for cooking. Though a perennial it is not completely hardy in places other than the south-west and it is better grown as a half-hardy annual sowing the seed in boxes in the heated greenhouse in early spring. Like sage and thyme the leaves should be gathered early September just before fully ripened, "when the sap is full in the top of them" as one old writer put it.

The less tender Pot Marjoram, may be treated as a perennial and grown in the border if room in the herb garden is restricted.

There beloved of bees and butterflies it will give of its fragrant white flowers throughout late summer. The plant is propagated from cuttings or by division of the roots when necessary.

Mints. In my garden are growing a dozen different mints and what a joy they provide with their distinctive odours. Not everyone is used in the kitchen, but are highly prized in my fragrant garden, for there is scarcely an occasion when either the children or myself go into the garden and return without a sprig of one of these mints either between our teeth or in a pocket to provide fragrance for the next few hours. I have mentioned about the use of dried eau-de-Cologne mint for helping to bring on sleep, Black Peppermint and Pineapple mint will also do likewise. The Bergamot-scented mint too is most aromatic dried and hung about a room in muslin bags. Not nearly so much use do we make of these aromatic mints. They should be planted, quite apart from the herb garden, by an entrance or alongside a path, like the path in my late grandfather's garden, which was of crazy paving and planted with all these delightful mints. There they were allowed to run at will, pushing their stems through the cracks in the stone work and providing a rich aroma when trodden upon and what fun we used to have in removing a leaf of each variety to detect the different scents. These were the same mints as heard in the old London cries, "Come, buy my mints", for in those days their various flavours were greatly appreciated. Peppermint, though so useful in medicines, is equally valuable for fatigue as anyone who has gone off to sleep on a bank of peppermint will know; a Lemon mint, known to Culpepper as Orange mint, is a great delicacy as a conserve. The strongly flavoured Corn mint is used in preventing milk turning sour, in fact, all the mints have been prized for centuries to combat curdling not only of medicines, but of one's stomach. Perhaps if we ate more mint, indigestion would not be such a common complaint. An infusion of peppermint leaves and elder flowers is good for colds.

Other mints of interest are the Japanese mint, which is used for abstracting menthol; the very hot flavoured Ginger mint and the delicious Apple mint.

Unlike many of the hard wooded shrub herbs, which like a

well prepared but dry soil, mints favour one containing the maximum amount of humus capable of retaining moisture through the summer months. Unlike the shrub herbs too, it does best in slight shade. Many mint beds are nothing but an entangled mass of woody root from which come sprigs of small leaved foliage which is almost devoid of flavour. To obtain mint at its best, it should be divided and replanted into a fresh bed in alternate years and should be given a mulch of peat and rotted manure each October, whenever new beds are not being made.

Rosemary. We have already seen something of the legends connected with this lovely evergreen shrub which no garden was without until quite recent times. It is still in great demand for making eau-de-Cologne perfume. It is just as attractive to bees and butterflies as it is to people; it should be planted with buddleias in the shrubbery rather than in the herb garden. It grows particularly well near the sea where it may be used for planting a fragrant hedge. It is readily increased from cuttings taken and inserted in sandy soil in August.

The misty-blue flowers of the rosemary are loveliest in the early spring before the hot summer sun takes from the plant its misty or mysterious qualities. Then too, the flowers are more fragrant than at any time. Its ethereal qualities were known to Sir Thomas Moore, who wrote that "it is the shrub sacred to remembrance", indeed, it may be called the most English of all plants, a symbol of love and friendship through the ages.

Sage. Like all the woody herb plants, sage loves a dry, sandy soil and plenty of sunshine. It readily strikes from cuttings and grows equally easily from seed. It is a delightful plant, its rich purple-blue flowers during mid-summer giving the herb garden quite an exotic appearance, enhanced by its rich grey-green leaves. For stuffing it is still used in quantity, but few realise that boiling water poured on its freshly gathered leaves makes an excellent "tea". There is a variety which bears a pure white flower which is most attractive planted with the common purple-flowered variety. Leaves of sage mixed with vinegar and honey is a useful gargle for sore throats.

Southernwood. Given the delightful country name of lad's-love in many districts, this must be one of the most fragrant of all plants possessing a heavy lemon like perfume, whilst its feathery grey foliage makes it most attractive to plant in the herbaceous border with catmint and bergamot, their fragrance blending with that of the sickly sweetness of other plants to produce a most pleasing aroma. Especially is southernwood pleasing after a shower of rain on a day when the summer sun has baked the ground and made the plants warm.

For placing in drawers as a safeguard against moths, and for strewing the floors of old houses and churches there is no herb possessing a more pleasing aroma than this.

Tarragon. The leaves are very aromatic but if used carefully in the kitchen can provide a pleasing addition to the menu. It is used to make tarragon-vinegar and tartar sauce the aroma being quite unlike that of any other plant. It is perennial, but tender in exposed positions and should be given protection in winter.

Drying Herbs

As so many herbs, mint sage, thyme (which is described in the following chapter), lavender and others are so valuable when dried and bottled for winter use, a small drying room where the leaves can be placed on trays allowing free circulation of air though shielded from the direct rays of the sun, will enable one to obtain from them the maximum amount of perfume or culinary value. When dry, the leaves or flowers can be rubbed from the stems and placed in dry jars and securely corked, or in muslin bags for hanging about the home.

CHAPTER XIII

SCENTED CARPETING PLANTS

A SCENTED "lawn" is a delightful addition to a garden and where there is an odd corner to spare, a small herb "lawn" will provide hours of delight. But make it large enough to lie on in dry weather, at least 6 feet square, for the refreshing fragrance of the plants will only be appreciated to the utmost if one has time to take out a cushion on which to rest one's head and then to lie flat over the carpet of fragrant herbs. Pennyroyal and the trailing evening primrose, camomile and semi-prostrate thyme, can all be used but like all herbs they are only richly fragrant if they are given a dry, sunny position where they can be warmed by the summer sun. Then let this warmth penetrate through one's clothes, so that upon rising you smell like a packet of fragrant herbs which will keep fresh and aromatic the whole day through. Or if the days of relaxation in the sun are gone, then use the "lawn" for walking on, tread the plants as much as you like and enjoy their rich perfume as the leaves and stems are crushed.

A fragrant path may also be made with these plants or just with camomile, which will quickly become matted and reveal no soil whatever. It will give off its fragrance whenever trodden upon and its pale green feathery foliage will be pleasing to behold. It was Falstaff who said of this plant "the more it is trodden upon, the faster it grows", and it must have been a plant well known to Shakespeare for it is native to our shores and was during Elizabethan days used for medicinal purposes. Parkinson tells us that "the flowers boiled in posset provoketh sweat which helpeth to expell colds and other aches". He describes its fragrance as like that of featherfew, refreshingly aromatic. It used to be said by old gardeners that a few plants of camomile about the garden, planted between crazy paving or on a dry bank would ensure the good health of all the other plants in the garden. But then camomile was thought to be a cure for almost all troubles of the body. It was steeped in boiling water as a cure for headaches and sweetened with honey was said to be a certain cure for sleepnessness. The leaves were also dried and smoked in pipes by those who suffered from asthma. It was of course the most important plant in the garden, yet today it is rarely seen and whether or not its value as a medicinal plant is thought to be in doubt, its fragrance in the garden is greatly refreshing. Its botanical name is *Anthemis nobilis*, and it bears masses of small white flowers. The plants are set 6 inches apart if it is required to use them for a "lawn" when they will quickly form a matted surface and will withstand the hardest wear. The more an established camomile "walk" is used the stronger and more matted the plants become and on a quiet day their fragrance is almost overpowering though refreshingly so.

Another mat forming plant bearing red clover-like blooms and possessing the delicate sweet fragrance of a pea flower is *Anthyllis montana*, the Mountain Vetch, which actually is a member of the pea family. The plants thrive in cold, poor soils and may be used for carpeting a bank used with camomile and other matted plants. The leaves are attractively covered with down, the small clover-like heads held on 2-inch stems, appearing late in June.

I purposely omitted the thymes from the chapter on herbs so that they could be included in this chapter, for to me they are plants more at home amidst crazy-paving stones and planted on sunny banks than ever they are in the herb garden. Or on a dry wall they are most charming. The fragrant, refreshing lemon thyme, far too aromatic a plant to be confined even to the herb garden. Then *Thymus coccineus*, which forms mats of grey-green leaves and deep crimson flowers which are most colourful planted between weathered stones. "I know a bank where the wild thyme grows", wrote Shakespeare, this the richly aromatic *Thymus serpyllum*, a native of our downlands, so loved by bees. Of this wild thyme there are a number of lovely varieties of which *R. coccineus* is one. Another is *T. lanuginosus*, which has woolly grey leaves, whilst Pink Chintz, bears flowers of the purest shell pink. Lovely for trough gardens is the tiny form *T. minimus*, which is deliciously fragrant. In addition to these lovely carpeting thymes, the dwarf woody kinds also possess a strongly aromatic perfume. Probably the finest of all is *T. argenta*, Silver Queen. This is the variegated leaved variety of the lemon-scented thyme, and it retains its foliage during winter. The variety *T. aureus*, smells strongly of *Verbena* and the foliage turns a rich golden colour in autumn. Most of the thymes reached Britain from the shores of the Mediterranean countries, where they could bask in long hours of sunshine, which brings out their full fragrance. Two interesting species from Corsica are *Thymus Corsicus*, which is of almost creeping habit and is strongly peppermint scented. The other is *T. herba barona*, charmingly named for in olden times it was used for rubbing into Baron of beef, its scent of carroway seeds giving the most delicious of all aromatic flavours to use with meat.

A charming thyme for making an edging to a herb garden or for planting on a dry wall is *Thymus carnosus*, which grows upright like a miniature Irish yew, the foliage carrying a strong aromatic scent. Another of similar habit is *T. fragrantissimus*, which has silvery-grey foliage very powerfully scented. Those who are about to lay out a new garden, may like to make a small Elizabethan knot garden for their herbs or for spring or summer bedding plants and there is no better plant for dividing these tiny miniature gardens than these upright thymes.

The culinary use of thyme is well known, it is indispensable to the housewife as is sage and mint. It should be picked during late summer just before it reaches its richest fragrance and is dried, like sage in an airy room. But do not use all of it for the kitchen, pick a few sprigs from each variety, tie the ends together and hang up a bunch in every room in the house, or mix up a pot-pourri of the dried leaves with those of sage and rosemary, and place the small bowls about the home, so that you can enjoy their refreshing perfume during the winter time.

The best method of increasing the plants is to insert

cuttings 2-3 inches long in a cold frame, or in boxes containing sandy soil. They will quickly root if inserted in August and will make sturdy little plants for setting out the following April.

I have not mentioned about the great pleasure to be obtained from many of these thymes, when planted in a window-box. Plant them with the scented geraniums, especially the lemon-scented varieties and enjoy the refreshing perfume throughout the summer.

A charming plant of creeping habit for planting midst crazy paving is Pennyroyal, *Mentha pulegium*, which bears a pretty little lavender coloured flower and dark shiny green leaves. In connection with this plant Parkinson has some interesting comment to make on the people and customs of his day. After telling us that Pennyroyal was good "to expell the cold thin phlegm from the lungs", and that it was also good "to comfort the stomach to stay vomiting," he goes on to tell us that "the former age of our great-grandfathers had all the hot herbs both for their meats and medicines, and therewith persued themselves in long life and much health, but this delicate age of ours doth wholly refuse these and therefore cannot be partaker of the benefit of them." Thus the decline of the use of herbs in the kitchen and for medicine had begun with Elizabeth dead but several years. Certainly it was used in large quantities during Tudor times for purifying water for drinking and Frances Bardswell tells us that during Elizabethan days "the herb was thought worthy of a place in posies that were given and accepted by lovers".

Parsley, though used entirely as a herb for culinary purposes, is a delightful plant for an edging to a flower bed, used in the same way as the aromatic featherfew. It is attractive when planted by the side of crazy paving, the bright curled green leaves being in marked contrast to the dull grey of the stonework. But the plant favours a rich, deeply dug soil and there is an old country saying that the seeds when sown "go nine times to the devil" before germinating. In some parts it is thought parsley seed will germinate only if sown on Good Friday, whilst in Derbyshire, it is thought that ill fortune will overtake a house where parsley is transplanted. The best parsley is only obtained by thinning out the seedlings to 6 inches apart so that the plants have room to develop and will produce those large well curled leaves held erect. As common as it is in the garden there is no more pleasing taste than that of parsley, whilst crushed in the hands its aroma is most refreshing.

An uncommon little plant, like a small heather and growing to a height of only 3 inches is *Micrimeria Corsica*. It bears minute pale grey foliage and pretty purple flowers, like those of heather. The foliage possesses the heavy fragrance in incense rather like that of rosemary. This is a first-class plant for planting amidst crazy paving or on the top of a dry wall for it can tolerate very dry conditions.

Another interesting plant for similar planting is the trailing evening primrose, *Oenothera missouriensis*, a native of the States of Missouri and Texas. The lovely pale yellow blooms are so freely produced that they may be said to cover the stones with gold, whilst the short stems that hold the blooms are attractively covered with down. Like most, but not all of the evening primroses, the blooms are at their best in the late evening when they are pleasantly scented. The plant likes a moist, rich loam, but does not appear too happy in a cold, clay soil. Propagation is by division or from cuttings inserted in boxes of sandy soil in May.

One of the most charming plants for planting amidst crazy paving stones is the easy but little known *Onosma tauricum*, which throughout summer bears its heads of amber-coloured tear-drop blossoms which are deliciously almond scented. The plant likes a sunny position and a well-drained loam, where it will soon make a large clump, and bears its deep golden blooms on 6-inch stems from June until the end of summer. Adding to its attraction is the grey-green evergreen foliage and stems which are covered with tiny hairs. Not without reason did Robinson write of it as being "amongst the finest of hardy flowers" nor has it become known as the Golden Drop plant. Deliciously fragrant during the daytime, its distinct almond perfume is even richer during early evening. I know of no lovelier plant, it grew to perfection in my old town garden before the war, planted between crazy paving stones over a bed of almost pure clay. Peat was packed round the roots at planting time and though the crazy paving was frequently submerged with rain water, due to its low lying position the onosmas quickly made large spreading plants and retained their vigour over the years. The plant was introduced from the mountains of Greece at the beginning of the nineteenth century and for half a crown there is no more charming plant and yet it is so rarely seen.

It is quite remarkable how many of the best plants for the crazy paving "garden" possess a rich fragrance and the lovely androsaces, are no exception. Two species I know that bear fragrant blooms are *A. arachnoidea superba*, which forms rosettes and dainty heads of pure white flowers in early May; and *A. chamaejasme*, which is known as the Rock Jasmine. This species produces large rosettes of fringed leaves and white blooms on 3-inch stems and they carry the delicate perfume of the winter jasmine. These two species are easy to grow and are extremely hardy and like the onosma and the trailing evening primrose, will prove ideal rockery plants in addition to their value for positions where their almost prostrate habit is required.

The Himalayan androsace, *A. lanuginosa*, is of even more trailing habit. Like the onosma, its stems and foliage are covered with hairs which give the plant an attractive downy-grey appearance. The blooms are produced in small rounded heads and are of a delicate rose-pink colour, faintly perfumed. This species is not altogether hardy except where it is grown in sight of the sea and of course the milder climate of the west. It likes a sunny position as do all the androsaces and a well drained sandy loam.

The fragrant Daphnes possess great charm. For the shrub border *D. mezereum* and its close relations are known to, and loved by many gardeners; but the dainty Garland Flower, *Daphne oneorum*, which grows to a height of only 6-8 inches is deserving of great recognition. One attractive peculiarity it possesses is that it blooms twice each year, the first time in May, then again late in September, bearing honey-scented deep pink flowers in clusters at the end of each shoot. The

plant is of trailing habit forming cushion-like clumps of evergreen foliage and so is ideal for a dry wall or for crazy paving.
Another dwarf Daphne, *D. Blagayona*, produces its clusters
of richly fragrant white blossoms on only 4-inch stems. The
blooms persist well into summer and are enjoyed by bees.
Quite as dwarf in habit is *Daphne striata*, which produces
deep pink flowers in June. They are almost as fragrant as
honeysuckle. The white form, *striata alba*, is perhaps even
lovelier and just as fragrant. A species bearing not quite so
strong a perfume is the Rock Daphne, *D. rupestris*, which
forms thick mat-like foliage and bears large, waxy, pale pink
flower heads on short stems. It is slow growing and may take
two years to form a plant 12 inches in width, but it is well
worth waiting for. It likes a dry, stony soil, one containing
plenty of coarse sand and dislikes disturbance when once
established. These dwarf Daphnes are amongst the loveliest
plants of the alpine garden or lawn, they are thoroughly happy
amongst the thymes for they like the same dry, sunny
conditions, and for a dry wall or for crazy paving they
will be amongst the most fragrant of all summer flowering
plants.

Nor must we forget the semi-prostrate pinks for the paving
"garden"; *Dianthus alpinus*, with its dark, glossy green leaves
and large rich pink blooms deliciously clove scented. And the
Maiden Pink, *D. deltoides*, which covers itself with dainty rose-
pink blooms during mid-summer. One of the loveliest of all
is a new hybrid called Ariel, which forms neat round clumps
and bears richly perfumed flowers of vivid pink. Yet another
is *D. Boydii*, of prostrate habit and which bears large, sweetly
fragrant pink flowers. It is the longest flowering of all the
prostrate pinks.

I wonder how many know that charmingly fragrant little
plant the Calamintha, which forms neat tufts and bears its
large lilac blooms throughout summer and how aromatic they
are especially after a shower. This is certainly a plant for
carpeting, planted either on a bank of sandy soil or amongst
crazy paving stones. Like most carpeting plants it requires
a dry soil to bring out its rich perfume. In olden days the rich
menthol perfume of the blooms was much appreciated and the

plant was given the name of Cala, good and mintha, mint on account of its strong fragrance. The species, *C. suaveolens*, which is slightly taller growing has attractive grey foliage and flowers of rich purple, a plant of great charm but so little used in the garden.

CHAPTER XIV

WINTER FRAGRANCE

AT no time of the year is colour and fragrance in the garden more welcome than during the dull winter days and quite apart from the scented bulbs, it is surprising how many of the winter flowering plants possess perfume. Rosemary should always be planted for the leaves retain their fragrance the whole year round and no plant is more rooted in our history than this. It is said that sprigs of rosemary were used to adorn the hair of Anne of Cleves at her marriage to Henry VIII, and right up to the turn of the present century most brides carried a sprig in their posies, and no honey is more deliciously flavoured than that where the bees have made use of the flowers of the rosemary. Rosemary loves the shelter and dryness of a wall so where possible plant the shrub at the foot of a wall, under the eaves of a house will be admirable and with it plant the interesting bush honeysuckle, *Lonicera fragrantissima,* which in mid-January covers itself in a mass of drooping white blossoms which carry the true heavy honeysuckle perfume. It will make a bush up to 8 ft. tall and quickly reach the same height if planted and trained up a wall or arch. If possible do plant it close to the house, for if given some protection from the worst of the weather, the plant will remain in bloom over a long period and will provide a continuous supply of fronds for home decoration and fragrance. Or plant it with the witch-hazel, *Hamamelis mollis,* against or amongst the dark foliaged evergreens which will show up their brightly coloured blooms to perfection, and will at the same time, provide some protection for the plants which are, of course, perfectly hardy even in the most exposed districts, but it is a pity to see their blooms battered by strong winds when at their loveliest. Those who have grown *Lonicera purpusi*, also winter flowering, say that whilst it is of neater habit than *L. fragrantissima*, and equally free flowering, it may not, in the north be quite so hardy. The flowers are pale creamy-white and strongly perfumed and I await with interest to see what it can do in my exposed garden.

All the witch-hazels are charming winter flowering plants though as I said in Chapter II, *Hamemelis Virginiana* is possibly the most outstanding. The first to come into bloom is *H. mollis*, which in my garden is in flower at Christmas. It appears to be more free flowering than the other species and covers its bare stems with masses of twisted golden-yellow blooms. As the plants are rather slow growing, rather than cut the sprigs for indoor decoration, E. T. Cook in *The Gardens of England* (1908) makes a delightful suggestion which I have always followed. That is to remove the individual blossoms of the various species as they open from December until March and to place them close together into saucers containing damp sand. Always kept moist and in a room which is not too warm, the blooms will remain fresh and fragrant for at least a fortnight and a saucer should be in every room of the house throughout the winter.

A lovely Hamamelis to flower from late January until March is *H. arborea rubra*, which will eventually make quite a large bush 6 ft. tall or more. The blooms are different in form and colour from the other species, being almost orange coloured and set in attractive burgundy-coloured cups. Another species of considerable charm is *H. vernalis*, from the U.S.A. It bears masses of small, very strongly perfumed bright red blooms during late winter but has the additional attraction in that its foliage turns a vivid yellow colour late in autumn. Its arched branches being clothed in beautiful grey green leaves during summer it is a most valuable plant for any garden. The witch-hazels need a peaty or humus laden, slightly acid soil where they will make large plants in a reasonable time. They never seem to do much in a shallow, dry chalky soil.

Requiring similar conditions is the sweetest scented of all winter flowering plants, the wintersweet, *Chimonanthus fragrans.* It bears its pale yellow and purple flowers from mid-November and during the bleakest days of winter on leafless stems and indoors is more fragrant than any plant. The blossom is able to withstand any amount of rain, frost or snow, but unless given the protection of a wall may be damaged by strong winds. There is a large flowered variety called Grandiflorus, which is possibly even more sweetly perfumed.

West Country gardeners will find the Lemon Verbena, *Aloysia citriodora,* a magnificent plant. It is one of the few plants to bear a scented flower as well as fragrant foliage, which will scent the winter air for some distance if planted in the shelter of a walled garden. It must be given a poorish soil, some humus by all means, but no manure, and so as not to make too much soft growth, it should be kept as dry as possible. Like most tender plants it seems to be hardy on the sea coast if given a sheltered position and its roots are covered with ashes during winter. It should be treated as a wall plant for it makes rapid growth and the pale green leaves are most attractive as a background for other plants.

The ancient bay tree should also be grown for the fragrance of its leaves. Poet's Laurel or Sweet Bay, it is called, but really it is a member of the laurel family, *Laurus nobilis,* which William Robinson tells us in *The English Flower Garden* should be planted on a dry, sunny bank, where it will thoroughly ripen its shoots and prove both hardy and aromatic the whole year round. But Robinson should have gone further and suggested planting it amongst the hardier Portugal laurel, or amongst some shrubs which will provide just a little protection, for growing entirely unprotected as it is so often in a tub at the entrance to a house, the leaves may become browned if the frosts are severe. Such plants growing in tubs are best wintered under an open shed or may be covered with a sack.

The Romans appreciated perfume and because the leaves of the bay were so pleasantly aromatic they were always used to garland the triumphant warrior or athlete. In mediaeval gardens of England it was grown for simmering and making a tonic for the hair and later the leaves were used for flavouring milk puddings as an alternative to nutmeg. From ancient times too, the branches were used with those of rosemary, holly and mistletoe for Christmas decorations in church and home, probably to counteract the damp, musty smell of the earth or stone floors. Several sprigs tied with dried lavender and the green sprigs of rosemary and hung in the bedroom during winter will instil sleep with their aromatic fragrance.

The lovely Viburnums and Daphnes we have already mentioned, but another lovely shrub which is completely hardy in all gardens is the Japanese Quince, *Cydonia Japonica*, and its many lovely varieties, introduced to our gardens at the beginning of the nineteenth century. Of all shrubs I think this is my favourite and nowhere is it used to better advantage than planted against a low wall bordering or surrounding a lawn. More accurately it should be classed as early spring rather than late winter flowering for it blooms from early March until well into April. The great value of the plant is not only its ability to bear its clusters of flowers, shaped like the wild rose, in abundance, but in its habit of growing as wide as it does tall. It is therefore ideal for covering a wall which it will quickly do if its side shoots are encouraged rather than its upward branches. Again, its pale yellow fruits of autumn not only lend colour to the garden, but may also be used for a fragrant jelly. Besides the true *C. japonica*, which bears masses of delicately scented deep pink flowers, one of the best is called Crimson and Gold, which is a strong grower bearing rich blood red flowers. With it *C. alba*, of purest white, is a delightful contrast. Slower growing is Knap Hill Scarlet, whose blossoms are of a brilliant orange-red.

In a garden in Cheshire almost on the coast, I recently saw growing the camphor plant, *Camphorosma Monspeliacum* and was delighted with its heavy camphor odour carried by the wood and foliage. It is evergreen and makes a low shrub and would appear to be an ideal foil for the brightly coloured dwarf daphnes. It is a fragrant plant, not in my own garden as I have a feeling it might be too exposed, for the coastal districts of Cheshire and Lancashire are in comparison quite warm, strange as it may seem. It is however a plant for the connoisseur, its fragrance during winter being quite astounding.

There are two charming Camellia species, which bloom in winter. *C. oleifera*, bears richly perfumed white blooms during January, whilst *C. Sassanqua rubra*, produces its deep rosy-red blooms during November and December. To prolong the period, the species *C. Williamsi Lanarth*, which should be grown against a wall bears its rich shell-pink bell-shaped blooms early in March. In the south they are quite hardy throughout most winters but if planted north of Gloucester they should be given a sheltered corner preferably under a wall and the roots should be covered with ashes in October.

An evergreen fragrant foliage plant which makes a dainty, slender bush and bears in summer large white flowers which have dark blotches at the base of each petal, is the Gum Cistus, of the same race as those pretty little shrubby rock roses we plant so much in rockeries. All of them, including *Cistus ladaniferus*, whose foliage remains aromatic throughout the winter, like a stony soil, preferably in full sun where they will bloom to their heart's content. The Gum Cistus, like the others, may readily be increased by striking the heeled cuttings in frames of sandy soil in late summer.

Indispensable for the shrubbery or wild garden is the Oregon Grape, which sounds most sophisticated, but which is really only our valued friend, the *Berberis aquifolia*, a plant which does well under the tallest and most densely leaved of all forest trees, remaining colourful the whole year round and providing its shining, rich green foliage as an attractive foil for chrysanthemums. Towards the end of winter, in early March, the foliage which now has turned almost purple in colour combines with the bunches of rich golden flowers to make yet another attractive indoor display. The flowers too are very sweetly scented and the foliage and stems possess that pleasant woodland fragrance which is equally attractive when brought indoors.

The chrysanthemum must not be forgotten, though today it is such a specialist's crop that, like the dahlia, it demands a book entirely to itself. And few will agree that it is a flower with perfume, though I refuse to believe there is no fragrance in its foliage even if it is not a sweet fragrance. The rich, musty aroma of chrysanthemums is only enjoyed when the blooms are cut and taken indoors and is there a more autumny aroma than they give, and if the borders contain masses of those delightful Korean hybrids, the bloom and aroma may be enjoyed in both garden and home right up to Christmas, when heavy rain and lack of sunshine tends to make the blooms become faded. But the Koreans are extremely hardy and may be classed as late autumn and early winter flowering plants and the roots may be left in the ground the whole year round and divided in alternate springs. The plants should be staked in the summer to prevent their being blown about by early autumn winds, but otherwise will need no further attention. As is necessary with other chrysanthemums there is no need to disbud nor to lift the plants for indoor flowering when the weather becomes cold and damp. Chrysanthemums must surely remind one that the end of summer and the warm days are at an end for yet another year, a sad time possibly, but to those who possess a garden however small, may continue to enjoy colour and fragrance until spring comes once again. And if one is fortunate to live in the country, there the room fragrant and warmed by the burning of apple wood, will bring out the rich aroma of indoor chrysanthemums.

Following the great work at Otley by the Simpsons, hybridising the Korean chrysanthemums, in the 1930s, we now know them as the Otley Koreans, like the original Russell Lupins, being natives of Yorkshire. There is a wide range of magnificent colours from which to choose, from the brilliant orange, double-flowered Cheerfulness, through the coppery-rose-coloured Margaret Simpson and the dusky pink Teresa, to the rich yellow-coloured Sun Gold. But perhaps the three best varieties for a small garden are Pauline, rich salmon-apricot; Startler, deep claret-pink; and Cavalier, brightest scarlet. All are dwarf, growing to a height of 2 ft. and are of extremely bushy habit. They make lovely pot plants too, covering themselves with bloom and remaining colourful from September until early December.

No garden is complete without its Christmas Rose and what

a grand plant this is, hardy, with pleasant foliage during summer and producing its glorious pink-white blooms during the depth of winter and what a delicious perfume they carry. In a cool room the blooms will remain fresh in water for almost a fortnight and are never more attractive than when placed floating in a large bowl. Planted beneath trees or shrubs or in a corner sheltered from the prevailing winter winds, the plants will bloom profusely year after year, in fact, like the peony, when once established, the plants hate disturbance.

The best time for planting is September and if space is limited even a single plant set in a corner beneath a wall will provide an abundance of bloom in even the most exposed garden, but make certain that the soil is well drained so that excess moisture will not hang around the plants during winter, and yet some humus is essential to keep the soil moist during summer. Old mushroom manure and peat is ideal. To ensure buds opening in time for Christmas table decoration, it is advisable to cover the plants with a cloche or to place small sheets of glass round the plants early in November. Cloches will also keep the blooms clean.

Of *Helleborus niger*, the true Christmas Rose, there are several forms, the first to come into bloom being *H. altifolius*, which bears large blooms on tall stems in November. Madame Fourcade, of purest white, follows in December with the lovely Irish variety, St. Brigid. The largest amount of bloom which reaches the florists during December and January is from plants known as the Bath Variety, so named for it was in the nineteenth century grown in large quantities around Bath to provide the elegant townspeople with a corsage for the Christmas season.

Few gardens now seem to grow that wonderfully hardy and colourful polyanthus, Barrowby Gem. With its almond perfume and attractive blooms of pale yellow, shaded green, this is surely one of the most charming of all winter plants ideal for a window-box, on the rockery, or planted about a shrubbery or woodland garden. And as an edging to a path or border it remains colourful from early February until spring gives way to summer. I have seen the plants come into bloom during the bleakest weather, but when an hour of midday winter sun has melted the ice and given of its almost negligible warmth. That is sufficient for Barrowby Gem to open its blooms which are held on strong polyanthus stems. If cut and taken indoors the frilled blooms will remain fresh for at least a fortnight and they retain their fragrance the whole time. In a window box facing south, the plants will remain colourful throughout winter and will be enhanced if planted with some of the extremely hardy winter flowering pansies. Barrowby Gem was raised by a Mrs. McColl, in Scotland I believe, which would account for its hardiness. During recent years it is said that it is losing vigour and in fear of dying out like several of the old double prim-roses, but my own plants, obtained from a Cheshire farm, where the plants had always been given plenty of manure, grow as large and as strong as cabbages.

The little winter pansies which are more like violas are really free flowering during winter and from a sowing made outdoors in early July, will commence to bloom late in October and continue throughout the winter and spring. They make delightful window-box subjects planted with early flowering crocus or the hardiest of the primroses. A particularly attrac-tive combination is to plant the variety Wine Red, with polyanthus Barrowby Gem. Equally charming is to use the rich velvet purple coloured variety March Beauty, with Barrowby Gem and for later flowering plant a few roots of Craddock's White, also sweetly perfumed. There is a large range of the winter flowering pansies all carrying the sweet fragrance of freesias. Helios is rich yellow; Celestial Queen, pale blue; and the pure white, Snowstorm, is the hardiest of all, blooming during the severest of winters and even through the thick fogs of our cities.

With the scented blooms of *Berberis aquifolia*, the winter may be thought to be behind, however cold the early spring winds may be. The blackthorn and the pussy willow and the first daisies are signs that warmer days may be expected and soon the cherry blossom will cover the trees in snowy raiment, Kent and Worcestershire being the first of the counties to be reborn. Then will follow the apple blossom, scenting the orchards of the West Country from Gloucester to Penzance, but though the pink-garbed trees are so eagerly awaited, we do not forget those shrubs and plants which have kept our spirits up during the bleak days just passed, both in the garden and in the home the fragrance of their bloom will have comforted us.

CHAPTER XV

AROMATIC FRUITS

IS there a more delightful part of the garden than the orchard and the fruit garden? Here there is fragrance almost all the year round and I would rather have an orchard than all the flower borders imaginable. When living in a small white-washed Somerset cottage surrounded by a mixed orchard, one experienced an ever delightful fragrance from Christmas right through the year. It was always our aim to pick fresh apples from the tree on Christmas morning and anyone who has removed the yellow-russeted Claygate Pearmain, covered with feathery white frost will have yet to enjoy the English apple at its best. The coldness brings out its aromatic perfume as nothing else can do and this is an apple which remains crisp and tight skinned until spring, though it is best to remove the fruit before the more severe January weather. This was a glorious orchard in all stages of growth, in spring it was carpeted with the fragrant wild daffodil, then came primroses and cowslips in drifts of various shades of yellow and gold. The bedroom windows opened above a sea of pink and white blossom of apple, pear and plum trees mingled with the grey fairy-like blossom of the damsons. There was the large, flat, pink blossoms of that grand cooking apple Arthur Turner, and the sweetly scented blossom of Brownlee's Russet. The rich crimson blossoms of several of the old cider apples, now also being planted no more, for a new generation of gardeners in the West Country prefer their insipid beer to the heavily aromatic cider which their fathers loved. And so names with such a decidedly West Country flavour as Knotted Kernel, Woodbine Sweet Alford, Striped Beefing and Brabant's Bellefleur, must surely soon pass from our language.

Used for windbreaks about the large orchard were the gnarled trees of damsons and bullaces, Merryweather and Farleigh Prolific, both abundant croppers but just as valued for their blossom in springtime. Then the beautiful honey-scented blossom of the pears, pure white with dark anthers, and what wonderful colourings the leaves assume in autumn. The bright yellow of Josephine de Malines and Jargonelle, the orange of Conference, the crimson of Pitmaston Duchess and the difficult Seckle, the sweetest and most musky flavoured of all pears.

For a few weeks in June and July the orchard lost its fragrance and its colour, but then we had beds of deliciously fragrant strawberries, bushes of many of those old world gooseberries now alas almost extinct, and to follow in August were rows of tall raspberry canes covered with luscious aromatic berries. Their fragrance could be enjoyed many yards away, at times and especially after a day's rain, when the fruit could not be picked the aroma was overpowering.

The gooseberry reached its peak a century ago when there were several hundred varieties in cultivation. Almost a hundred survive to this day though present day gardeners know no more than half a dozen noted for their cropping powers rather than for their flavour. Those who do not know the aromatic pale green berry of Glencarse Muscat are missing a great pleasure. Another of rich flavour is Gunner, which bears a large, deep green berry attractively striped with yellow.

A superb old gooseberry called Hebburn Prolific, described by Dr. Robert Hogg in *The Fruit Manual* written in 1860, as being "very rich and sweet; an abundant bearer" is perhaps the most delicious in my collection of nearly seventy varieties. Why it has been allowed to become almost extinct is a mystery.

Most gooseberry enthusiasts agree that for rich flavour the yellow varieties take some beating, and of these a grand variety for the small garden is Pilot, which makes a compact, neat bush and bears a profusion of long, hairy, bright yellow berries which if allowed to remain on the bushes until completely ripe, will perfume the air all around. Another yellow of aromatic flavour is Langley Beauty, introduced in 1896, so may be said to be a "new" gooseberry. The skin of the fruit is almost transparent, whilst the berries are sweet and highly flavoured. At the same time Messrs. Veitch gave us Langley Gage, the small white, hairy berries are said to be the richest flavoured of all. Another white of superb eating qualities is Whitesmith, first known to gardeners in the year of Waterloo, and still a commercial favourite. The huge white fruits are covered with down and are exceedingly aromatic when fully matured, like eating nectar. No fruit garden is complete without a red gooseberry and none is of more delicious flavour than Champagne Red, which bears a hairy, bright red berry said by Hogg to be of "very rich flavour, vinous and sweet". This is the children's favourite, for when really ripe they pop the berries into their mouths like sweets.

But the gooseberry comes again, this time in early autumn, with the rich yellow colourings and the autumnal fragrance of their leaves, which mingled with the dying strawberry and raspberry leaves provide possibly the most fragrant of all garden scents. I never know whether the loveliest perfume of all is the delicate woodland fragrance of the early spring flowers or the musky aromatic fragrance of the orchard and fruit garden in early autumn to be enjoyed when the air is still and the sun is sinking just before twilight comes. This is a mellow time, ripened pears and plums hang on the trees amidst an array of crimson and yellow leaves. Rarely are there any cold winds blowing as in springtime to take away the perfume of the dying leaves and of the fruits. The blackberries are there for the picking and mushrooms abound in the fields. From the kitchen their perfume whilst they cook, permeates right through the house. Francis Bacon appreciated the perfume of autumn leaves. In his essay *Of Gardens*, he describes the violet as producing the sweetest smell in the air, then "Next to that is the musk rose; then the strawberry leaves dying, with a most excellent cordial smell". But even more cordial is the rich pine perfume of the ripened fruit of the strawberry. If there are cricket grounds in heaven where the sun shines warm and the sound of bat and ball echoes through time eternal all well and good, if not, I can think of nothing better than to inhale the perfume of a large dish of almost ripe strawberries in a Somerset cottage, with the strains of Novello's "Glamorous Nights" seeping through the cob walls.

These West Country strawberries really do carry a perfume, quite overpowering at times. Of rich pine flavour is the new

Cambridge Early Pine, one of the first of all the strawberries, ripening in a good season before the end of May. The fruit is round and the surface highly polished which enables the rain and dew to run off easily. A strawberry producing a fragrant wedge-shaped fruit is Cambridge Regent, also early to mature being almost like an early Royal Sovereign, still unbeatable for its flavour and perfume. Deliciously rich and sweet, with a scent almost like Burgundy wine is Cambridge Late Pine, which is highly resistant to frost and mildew. The deep crimson fruit is ideal for bottling and for flans, for it retains its fragrance and also its rich crimson colour.

Several of the true alpine strawberries bear fragrant fruit and the foliage later takes on the true autumn colourings, which possess a rich aromatic scent. Perhaps the richest flavoured is Belle de Meaux, which bears a small crimson berry, but almost as aromatic is the white berried Delight, which forms no runners and is increased by division.

The new perpetual strawberries have by now become firmly established. They really will fruit right up to Christmas if cloches are used. Several varieties renowned for their high cropping powers are of inferior flavour, but one possessing rich pine flavour is Kuntner's Pineapple Triumph, which is also a heavy cropper. Another is Charles Simmen, which bears large crimson berries, extremely musky and equal in flavour to Cambridge Regent. Of excellent flavour too is St. Claude. The fruit is juicy and sweet, the berries being very large and glossy, like Cambridge Early Pine. During autumn when the fruit is maturing, its fragrance is increased by the perfume of the changing leaves. To prevent splashing of the fruit from rains it is advisable to cover the soil around the plants with dead bracken and this too will combine to increase the scent of the strawberry plot.

At the back of the strawberries are the raspberries, which also are highly aromatic throughout late summer and early autumn. There is no perfume quite like that of a ripe raspberry, which has been warmed by the August sun. Like black currants, almost all raspberries carry a rich fragrance, though in several varieties the perfume is outstanding. One such variety is Park Lane, the fruit possessing a pungent aroma, and it is richly sweet. It possesses other excellent qualities in that the fruit not only ripens over a long period but will hang on the canes almost like a gooseberry. A variety of recent introduction, Royal Scot, one of the first to ripen, is also strongly aromatic, the berries being large, deep crimson in colour, in flavour like matured port-wine. The leaves of these two raspberries turn brilliant yellow in autumn and remain on the canes until cut down to make way for new growth. Several varieties of gooseberries also possess the same ability to retain their leaves until late in the season, turning a rich golden colour which greatly enhances the garden display. Whinham's Industry and Rifleman, Leveller and Langley Beauty, all possess this quality.

The autumn fruiting raspberries also are famed for their aromatic fragrance. The colour of both fruit and foliage, still green, adds distinction to the fruit garden in autumn. Hailsham, an old favourite, bears its rich crimson fruit during late September. It is sweet and juicy and possesses a distinct perfume. A variety with the perfume of dried apricots is Lord Lamborne, now rarely seen. Strangely the colour of its fruit is deep golden-apricot, the leaves being deep bottle-green, a most wonderful sight during early October.

Blackcurrants too possess an attractive pungent fragrance. Rich in Vitamin C. and so useful for making blackcurrant tea for a winter beverage, this is one of the most valuable fruits of the garden. A "hedge" of blackcurrants will prove useful for providing the strawberry plot with some shelter, or will make a pleasant division between various parts of a garden. Perhaps the most outstanding variety is Laxton's Giant, which bears a pungently aromatic fruit the size of a black Early Rivers cherry. It is certain to take all the prizes at the local show. Whilst in the kitchen, it bottles and cooks well. But it is when taken from the bush and eaten like a dessert gooseberry that its distinctive aroma is most appreciated. A heavy cropping variety which bears a long truss of sweet and fragrant fruit is Mendip Cross, which like Laxton's Giant, is ready to pick early in July.

Retaining its fruit, if allowed to do so, until October is the new variety Laleham Beauty, the berries being richly perfumed and extremely sweet and juicy. This grand currant adds to the bountiful supply of autumn fruits, golden pears and rosy cheeked apples, autumn fruiting raspberries and strawberries, blackberries and the later maturing plums.

A handsome richly-aromatic plum is Laxton's Delight. It carries the popular greengage flavour and when really ripe in late September, the fruit is a deep golden-yellow colour, heavily speckled with red. Oullin's Golden Gage, is also a superb plum for September eating. The golden-green fruit is of richest flavour, which is just as delicious when bottled as when eaten straight from the tree. For early October eating the new plum, Severn Cross, bears a large handsome green, flushed pink fruit which carries a strong aromatic perfume when eaten. But as palatable as are these large plums, they surely fall short of the pungent flavour of damsons which are so essential for jam and bottling. The perfume of simmering damsons must rival that of blackberries cooking and mushroom boiled in milk as an autumn smell. The perfume is of dead bracken and decayed leaves, the true autumn fragrance. That grand damson called Westmorland, will remain on the tree until early December if necessary and will then still be suitable for any form of cooking.

But the perfume of autumn will not be complete without the blackberry and several of the hybrid berries, for not only does their fruit carry a rich aroma, but their dying leaves too. Plant them about the garden for screens or for hedges when they will return the little attention needed to tying up the shoots a hundredfold. Wonderful for a hedge is that vigorous grower Himalaya Giant, which produces its large richly flavoured berries in abundance. More handsome is the Parsley-leaved blackberry, the foliage of which turns the most arresting colours during autumn, whilst its fruit possesses a strong aroma. The Japanese Wineberry, with its fruit like a loganberry in colour though smaller and sweeter, is also a lovely plant for its bright crimson coloured canes look particularly warm and attractive in winter and retain their leafy fragrance all the year round.

Better than the old loganberry is the new thornless variety, which bears during late summer a huge dull crimson fruit which possesses the true aroma of the loganberry, but is much

sweeter and softer to eat. To bridge the gap between the loganberry and the true blackberries, the Lowberry should find a
place in every garden. It is a cross between these two fruits
and combines the better qualities of both parents, bearing a
fruit quite 2 inches in length of a shining jet black colour
and carrying the rich aroma of the blackberry.

Of apples that are perhaps more aromatic than others, the
old Devonshire Quarrenden, still a West Country favourite, is
still one of the best. It was grown in the west three hundred
years ago and was then planted for the beauty of its fruit,
deep crimson and yellow, and its grey foliage quite as much as
for its crisp, aromatic flavour. Though its fruit is by no means
handsome, the Essex favourite, D'Arcy Spice, which retains
its crisp freshness well into the New Year, makes superb
eating and is one of the most highly aromatic of all apples.
This is a yellow-skinned apple, spotted with russet and there
is no doubt about it but that the russets are richly aromatic.
There is that juicy little apple, St. Edmund's Russet, which
carries the perfume of a pear; Pineapple Russet, introduced in
1780, its small green and brown apples being attractively pine
flavoured; Egremont Russet, one of the most spicy flavoured
of all apples. Then for late eating, Orlean's Reinette, the best
of them all, the flesh being sweet and fragrant.

Over the winter there is always plenty of apple wood to
burn in the open fireplace, wood that has been cut from
decaying old trees or from trees blown down as the winter
winds sweep across the Plain of Sedgemoor. Gnarled branches
wrenched from the old trees of Devonshire Quarrenden, which
were said to be growing in the orchard whilst Monmouth was
fleeing from the Battle of Sedgemoor, not the same trees, but
of the same variety. And is there any more pleasant smell
than the burning of apple wood, unless it be that of peat, or
turf, as it is called in Ireland? Those who live in our cities
must have forgotten those delightful smells, for them the
harsh smells of coal, petrol and tar.

The countryman lives amongst the fragrance of the pine
woods, he treads the bracken and dried leaves of beech and
oak, he inhales the honey-scented blossom of the lime tree, the
hawthorne and the elder. Over the village in autumn hangs

the misty fragrance from burning peat and apple wood, for there are always supplies of these available in the West Country. But even there conditions are changing. Much of the wood is that from old cider orchards which will never be replaced whilst the open fireplace is giving way to the cooker fed with coke. Perhaps it is as well for soon there will be little more wood from the old orchards, for we drink beer instead of cider and the townsman prefers his imported apples to those of the English orchard. But then there will be the fruit garden to revive the spirits with its rich perfume from May until December and after that the aromatic pears and apples lying in store and holding inside their skins the sunshine of summer days for our winter enjoyment.

CHAPTER XVI

THE BUTTERFLY BUSH

FAR too long have the buddleias remained in the background of the shrubbery in more ways than one. No shrub is of greater value, especially in the new garden where it so quickly establishes itself, and where it makes the butterfly in its array of summer colours so welcome. The flowers too are sweetly perfumed. Because of its attraction to the butterfly, especially the Red Admiral, it is also known as the butterfly bush, but bees love it equally as well. The shrub best enjoys a rich loamy soil where its roots may be moist and cool throughout the summer and although it will flower and flourish in a position of semi-shade, it is at its best in full sunlight. Planted thus, it will rapidly reach a height of 10 ft. or more, its long arching branches and sprays providing more colour than almost any other shrub during that late summer period from mid-July until late in October when the brooms and mock oranges have long finished flowering. When once established the plants will literally cover themselves with their long sprays which produced against their grey-green foliage give an appearance of great charm. Against the window of my study I have one of the modern buddleias planted 2 ft. from the wall of the house, it is a variety of recent introduction called Charming, which bears the nearest to a true pink flower of all the buddleias and which carries a pleasing delicate perfume. Throughout late summer and early autumn on dry summer days the flower spikes are covered with butterflies, their colourful wings a sight of great charm against the pale pink of the flowers. The plant is indeed well named.

It is not generally realised that the buddleias make a most excellent and attractive hedge. Planted 3 ft. apart, they may be trained by cutting away all unnecessary growth during early April, leaving those branches that are necessary for closing up the gaps. Old wood may be thinned out every alternate year or just cut back to the height of the hedge which should have reached 5 ft. in two years. Such a hedge will act as an efficient and most attractive wind break and if planted alternately with as many as a dozen varieties will provide a display of colour of the greatest splendour over a very long period. What is more, the ability of the plants to retain some of their foliage and the dead flower spikes throughout winter, even if in a withered state, greatly increases their value as a windbreak. In my own garden, lashed by winds directly from the North Sea, the plants have been allowed to attain a height of 12 ft. which they rapidly reach. The variety used is the rich purple, Dubonnet, which are under planted with the less vigorous but equally attractive, White Bouquet, which is allowed to reach a height of no more than 6 ft. The contrasting colours make for a particularly delightful display and an efficient shelter hedge.

For a specimen plant for a sunny position by the side of a house or in the border, the plant should be kept in shape by careful cutting out of dead and unwanted wood during spring. Though I have never found the buddleia in any way tender, a slight tendency towards this may be exaggerated if pruning is done after flowering in late autumn. This may be possible in the south-west, but is not advisable for other parts of Britain where I have found that given spring pruning the plant is more vigorous in the exposed coastal areas of the far north than in the more sheltered positions of the south. It is said that the buddleia likes a lime-free soil. It will however flourish in any soil containing some humus by way of peat, leaf mould, decayed manure or spent hops, but it has been my experience that their colour, like that of the scabious, is enhanced by the addition of some lime rubble worked into the soil. Planting may be done any time from early November to the end of March, the most satisfactory plants being from small pots. No pruning should be done during their first year, just allow them to grow away at will, but until they are thoroughly established and should a severe winter be experienced, they will appreciate some protection round their roots in the form of bracken, straw or leaves. If it is necessary to keep the plants well within bounds in the small garden or overcrowded border, the plants may be cut to within 18 inches of ground level every April, otherwise pruning should consist of removing dead wood and the flowering spikes of the previous season. This buddleia is of the species *Davidii* or *variabilis*, a native of China and Tibet, a plant which fortunately for gardeners has received considerable attention from the hybridists during recent years, the modern varieties having improved out of all recognition from the pale mauve flowers, borne in short, thin sprays which we knew before the war. Several of the modern varieties have been mentioned. Others of charm and vigour are the rosy-coloured Pink Pearl; the huge pink and white sprays of Elstead; the deep purple-blue Ile de France; and the crimson-purple Royal Red. Another lovely white, possessing a delicate perfume is White Profusion, which covers itself with masses of long pointed sprays; and possibly the loveliest of all is the new powder-blue variety, Empire Blue. A variety having almost pure blue flowers and attractive dark grey foliage is the recently introduced Glasnevin Blue. Another of great charm is the rosy-mauve, Fascination. The plants under normal conditions will last a lifetime and the most expensive of them costs only a few shillings. What is more, they grow equally as well in the town garden as they do in country and coastal areas. The townsman with a wall of a garage or shed to hide will will find these buddleias will do the job rapidly and efficiently and be a joy to behold through late summer and autumn when the herbaceous border and shrubbery is past its best. As a background to a rose bed they are delightful or with them plant some of the modern michaelmas daisies to give some colour right through autumn.

A species which is excellent for planting against a wall, on account of its tall, weeping habit is *alternifolia*, which is very lovely with its silvery leaves and drooping mauve flowers which are also sweetly scented. This species too, is a great attraction for bees and butterflies which cover its yard long sprays throughout summer.

Two more species of the buddleia are worthy of planting though neither are so striking in form; nor do they attract butterflies in the same way as do *variabilis* and *alternifolia*. They are the interesting evergreen and sweetly scented *globosa,* which bears orange coloured flowers the size of a tiny orange during May and June and which requires any pruning to be done in autumn; and the winter flowering *auriculata,* which should be planted against a sunny sheltered wall for it is not quite hardy. The roots should be covered in a severe winter or in an exposed position. Throughout the coldest months it will bear its cream-coloured flowers which smell much like honeysuckle and are lovely for cutting and bringing indoors when they will spread their scent right through the house.

CHAPTER XVII

THE ROSE

OUR national flower since adoption by the first of the Tudors almost five hundred years ago and so valuable in its many forms and species for all gardens, in the scented garden the rose is indispensable. Recently there has been much correspondence in the gardening press as to the merits of fragrance in roses and carnations. Is it as important as some would have us believe? Evidently the raisers of new varieties do not think so for only a very small percentage possess any fragrance comparable with the old cottage Cabbage rose, and the Red Rose of Provence which grows to a height of 6 ft. and more down the narrow path of my Somerset cottage. It has been left to grow and bloom just as it pleases, unpruned, unstaked and there it bears masses of those ungainly blooms of a rich purple-crimson as fragrant as the strongest perfumed of the lilies. No hybrid teas grow with them, they are planted in beds to themselves for they would be out of place amongst these old roses, which produce a far stronger perfume when distilled than any other flower. Parkinson writes of the "thickness and doubleness of the great Provence rose"; no rose in fact possesses such a massive bloom and is of such strong constitution. The true Cabbage rose is of pink and cream shades similar in habit to the genuine Red Provence rose and almost equally as fragrant. There is also a pure white form of dwarf habit, not quite so powerfully perfumed, but which remains longer in bloom. I do not know whether this white form can still be obtained, but the old Red Provence rose may, even though it was known to English gardens during the sixteenth century. Equally fragrant is the vigorous Tour de Malakoff, which produces large blooms of shades of lilac and purple; and for a contrast plant the rich carmine-pink Duchess de Montebello of the same species.

Known to our gardens even earlier than the Provence rose

were the Gallica roses, a species described by Gerard in 1596 and which possess a powerful scent. This was the rose much admired in later years by the Empress Josephine of France and was much planted in her garden at Malmaison. These roses grow to a height of about 4 ft. and many possess an almost overpowering perfume. But none is lovelier nor is more fragrant than the old Apothecary's Rose, which bears a deep shell-pink bloom. Another attractive variety is known as Honorine de Brabant, the almost mauve-coloured blooms being striped with deeper mauve, the flowers being enhanced by the rich pale green foliage. For contrasting, the pure white, Quatre Saisous Blanc, is both charming and sweetly scented.

These Gallica roses will grow well in the poorest of soils so long as they receive some sunshine. They are rather like herbs for this reason and may be planted against a wall or used to cover an unsightly bank where they will flourish just as long as they receive some sunshine.

It is believed that this is the rose used by the House of Lancaster, adopted in 1277 by the son of Henry III, Earl of Lancaster, who was also Count of Champagne, where the Gallica rose is believed to have originated. This is thought to have been the rich crimson-purple rose, which is today known as Cardinal Richelieu, but it seems more likely that it was the deep crimson single variety which we now call Charles de Mills.

The House of York adopted Rosa alba which Gerard describes as bearing "faire double flowers, of a very sweete smell". It makes a handsome bush of up to 6 ft. tall with the leaves glossy like those of the yellow climbing rose, Emily Gray, and of a bottle green colour. The blooms too are most attractive, being shaped like flat saucers and possessing faint pink colourings and a distinct apple blossom perfume. Even lovelier is a variety called Koenigen von Danemarck, the blooms being of brightest pink and possessing a strong perfume. Another of charm is the old faintly pink, Maiden's Blush, the blooms being enhanced by the deep glossy green leaves. Indeed Miss Sackville-West, writing "In Your Garden" in the *Observer*, suggests that this really is the true Rosa alba, described by Gerard and she mentions that it holds its flowers longer than all other roses in her garden at Sissinghurst Castle, Kent.

For the old world garden, no rose is more attractive than the old Damask rose, introduced to our gardens with the return of the Crusaders and so often depicted in the floral paintings of early days.

"Gloves as sweet as Damask roses", wrote Shakespeare. The variety which produced its pink and white striped flowers during early summer known as York and Lancaster, may still be obtained. The blooms possess a pleasant sweet scent.

A rose noted for its apple-like scent is the Austrian briar, so valuable for using as a windbreak, but it is the leaves which emit the fragrance, not the blooms. The variety, Austrian Yellow, which bears masses of large, single clear lemon-yellow blooms, is always an attraction in the garden.

Probably derived from the old Provence roses are the strong growing moss roses which like a fairly moist soil to which has been added plenty of rotted manure. Under conditions they enjoy they will grow to a height of 5 ft. or more. All possessing a rich perfume it is surprising that from the fifty or sixty varieties grown in our gardens during the mid-eighteenth century, so few are obtainable today. The Common Moss rose is still with us, the shell-pink blooms being most attractively held in the pale green mossy cups and on long mossy stems. A rich coloured form is called Crimson Globe, the blooms being ball shaped. The old White Bath variety, dating from the year of Waterloo, is also still obtainable; the pure ivory-white flowers being large and fully double. Blanche Moreau, a variety of more recent introduction is also white and possesses a rich perfume. A striking variety is called Laneii, which bears large blooms of rich red.

I wonder if the old Crested Moss rose can still be obtained? By some it is said to be of the same order as the Cabbage or Provence roses and should really be classed as a Crested Cabbage rose. It was said by William Paul, writing a century ago to have been discovered growing in a wall in a convent garden on the borders of France and Switzerland, and I remember the attractive rosy-pink blooms and delicate perfume of a plant growing in an old cottage garden during the early 1930s, but it is rarely seen today.

Inheriting the delicate damask scent and the almost

perpetual flowering habit of the Tea rose, is the Bourbon rose, which reached us from France just a century ago. The large, flat, but fully double blooms are perhaps the loveliest of all roses and though first introduced to the Island of Bourbon near Mauritius, it was the gardener to the Duke of Orleans, who raised several of the lovely varieties we know today. The best is probably the large rose-pink Louis Odier, which blooms right through summer and autumn and is deliciously fragrant.

A superb variety, camellia-like in the shape of its bloom, is the double white Boule de Neige, whilst as a contrast the cherry coloured Charles Lawson is delightfully fragrant. But probably the best is the climbing form of the old Zephyrine Drouhin, which will so quickly cover a summer-house or the wall of a new house. The sweetly scented silvery-pink blooms are borne in clusters and in profusion throughout summer. It is a rose of outstanding beauty and what is more, it is thornless and so may easily be looked after. Another lovely Bourbon is the cream, flushed pink Madame Oger, which carries a rich fragrance and is at its best during late summer.

The China or Bengal roses are of fairly recent introduction and are sometimes known as the Monthly Roses on account of their flowering in flushes each month of the summer and autumn. They are much more compact than those previously mentioned rarely reaching a height of more than 3 ft. Introduced towards the end of the eighteenth century, and a great favourite in cottage gardens up to the First World War, was the lovely Blush China, a pale lilac-pink which seemed always to be in bloom. More striking though not in any way more charming is the vivid coppery-orange Comtesse du Cayla, which seems to be perpetually in bloom. One of the earliest to be introduced was the vivid crimson Madame Fabvier, which if planted with the old Blush China, will make a delightful low hedge being constantly in bloom and deliciously fragrant. Another of rich colouring is the rose, flushed gold Laurette de Messimy, which carries a distinct scent. The strongest scented of all is the pure white Rival de Paestrum, but in my garden I find the shrimp-like Hermosa equally as fragrant.

These hybrid China roses crossed with the Bourbons gave us the first Hybrid Perpetuals, which were in turn to become the parents of the hybrid tea roses we grow in profusion today. In late Victorian days the Hybrid Perpetuals were just as popular as the hybrid teas are today, but in spite of their name they fell from esteem on account of their shy blooming habit, though their flowers were larger and of richer colourings. One of the best of the Perpetuals is Mrs. J. Laing, a soft clear pink and extremely fragrant. Another was the brilliant scarlet, General Jacqueminot, and who amongst rose lovers has not at some time admired the large, pure white blooms of Frau Karl Druschki?

With each stage in the evolution of the rose we have been getting away from the full informal, fragrant flower to one which now only occasionally possesses any distinct perfume and which has become stiff and formal in habit. It is none the less attractive in its own way, but the lack of fragrance I deplore and from as many as a hundred modern varieties not more than twenty possess the rich fragrance we associate with the old Provence and China roses. The most fragrant of all the new roses are Charles Mallerin, which bears a bloom of black-crimson and which is not easily damaged by wind and rain, and Tahiti, of the well-known Peace habit, the rich primrose-yellow blooms having wavy petals and being attractively edged and flushed with gold and pink. The glossy green foliage and its freedom of blooming through the wet and windy summer of 1954 would make it the First rose in my garden, whilst it possesses the rich but refreshing perfume of the old Cabbage roses. One catalogue says it possesses a delicious apple scent and this is very near the mark. And yet, with all its toughness and delicious perfume, it has not yet become popular.

A new rose which may be said to possess the true apple perfume is that lovely bi-colour Forty-Niner, a most attractive rose the inside of the petals being velvety-red, the outside old gold, almost of a russet colour. And like Charles Mallerin, it does not quickly expand its bloom.

That grand old cerise, General McArthur, a descendant of one of the earliest of hybrid teas, the pink Caroline Testout, still popular though introduced more than fifty years ago, should be in every collection if only for its great freedom of flowering and rich Cabbage rose perfume. A pink rose rich in fragrance is the large flowered, The Doctor; whilst Verschuren's Pink is also sweetly scented and bears a bloom exceptionally neat in its early stages. Another pink, a silvery-pink, of fine form and habit is Rubaiyat, which makes a large bush and bears a full bloom which lasts well when cut.

Ena Harkness, rich crimson, we must not forget. It is the most free flowering of all roses, the strongly scented blooms being large and full. In my garden it is a far better rose than the popular Crimson Glory. It is a brighter scarlet, of much stronger constitution and does not suffer from mildew in a damp summer to the same extent as does Crimson Glory. Of other red roses, that possessing the most outstanding scent is Etoile de Hollande, which also makes a superb climbing rose.

Of yellow roses, several possess rich fragrance, the sort of scent that can be enjoyed without having to pluck a flower or having to bend down to detect its perfume as with most hybrid tea roses. Of these the new Sutter's Gold is very richly scented and bears a bloom of deep golden-yellow. That lovely rose, Golden Dawn, produces a bloom of pale moonlight yellow, which is deliciously fragrant whilst the cream-coloured Marcelle Gret carries a rich perfume long after it is cut.

Few white roses are strongly scented, the most outstanding being McGredy's Ivory, the blooms opening cream and possessing a distinct orange blossom scent.

The Floribunda roses are now great favourites on account of their freedom of flowering. They are the result of crossing the hybrid teas with the polyantha roses, with the resulting increase in the size of the blooms. But it is sad to recall that only few possess any perfume and that not very distinct. The crimson, Anne Poulsen, and the pink-flowered August See-vauer, both possess some scent, so does the scarlet, Commonwealth. There is a slight apple blossom perfume in the new white Irene of Denmark, from the House of Poulsen, but of all the others I can detect no distinct scent. In the true polyantha section, only the white Yvonne Rabier, which produces large trusses of bloom, seems to possess any perfume at all.

For the shrubbery, the old Musk Rose introduced into

England during Shakespeare's early days, is valuable for its fragrance. Shakespeare refers to it in *A Midsummer Night's Dream*:

> "Come, sit thee down upon this flowery bed
> While I thy amiable cheeks do coy,
> And stick Musk Roses in they sleek smooth head."

And in the seventeenth century the Musk roses were planted in most gardens. They flower first in early June then come again in early autumn and their great freedom of flowering and the fragrance of both bloom and foliage, their magnificent hips retained through winter give the briars an additional value in the garden.

Nor must we forget, for the trough garden or rockery, that charming miniature rose, Sweet Fairy, which bears tiny lilac-rose blooms of the richest perfume which cover the dainty little plants throughout summer.

And though we may plant the climbing Etoile de Hollande and Crimson Glory, to cover the walls of house and summer house, do not neglect those old-time favourites Gloire de Dijon, so richly perfumed and so long in flowering, and the pink and gold Madame Butterfly, also possessing rich perfume. Both are very old roses, Gloire de Dijon, being introduced more than a century ago, but they still hold their own in any company.

If the rose has a fault it is the tendency of the bloom to be so short lived. Robert Herrick, captured the fleeting spirit of the flower in his lines

> "Gather ye Roses while ye may,
> Old time is still a-flying,
> And the same flower that smiles today
> Tomorrow will be dying."

So plant them in quantity to enjoy them at their best and when making a choice is it too much to ask to give preference to those with perfume. A rose without fragrance is only half a rose, we miss its most attractive quality. The rose too, is essentially a cut flower, it does in fact last longer when indoors than it does in the garden and perfume in the house is just as enjoyable as in the open. And for pot-pourri they are indispensable. The petals of all those described are valuable, more especially the old Provence roses, the Damask roses and the richest scented of the hybrid teas, like Charles Mallerin and Tahiti. It is not possible in this little book to go into the making of pot-pourri in detail for this is a subject for a book on its own, but for those who are interested, here are one or two ways of using rose petals to provide fragrance in the home during winter.

This one is simple to make up. To a three-parts basinful of rose petals, which have been slowly dried in the house away from strong sunlight, add a cupful of dried thyme, rosemary and marjoram and the dried and crushed skin of an orange. Then add a few powdered bay leaves if they can be obtained, half an ounce of crushed cloves and a small teaspoon of Allspice. The whole should be well mixed and placed in a pot-pourri jar or bowl. The dried petals of the honeysuckle and the scented leaves of the geranium may be used instead but as with all perfumes, one which may be acceptable to a person who may enjoy a sweet, overpowering perfume may be unacceptable to one who enjoys a more refreshing fragrance. An alternative to the pot-pourri suggested would be to use the petals of the less powerfully scented roses and to these, in the quantity described, the dried petals of lemon thyme and the lemon-scented geranium leaves may be added. The dried skin of a lemon would replace that of an orange. Southernwood and verbena could also be added and a pinch of powdered nutmeg which would contribute to the refreshingly potent perfume.

Those who favour more of a sweet scent could add the leaves of the Dusky pink and of orange blossom and violets. It is all a matter of taste.

To make a moist pot-pourri, which will be even more powerfully fragrant, begin by placing a 6-inch layer of rose petals, undried into an earthenware jar. Cover with a thin layer of salt and leave to settle. Then as the season advances add the petals of orange-blossom, pinks, lavender flowers, more rose petals and each time covering with a layer of salt and keeping the jar quite closed. Finally some dried orange skin mixed with a quarter ounce of dried cloves and some dried marjoram. Keep closed until whenever the perfume is to be enjoyed.

Rose leaves may be made into little bags to scent clothes and bedding. The leaves are slowly dried, mixed with lavender and a few powdered cloves and made up into bags as soon as dry.

Pink rose-water is made by filling a saucepan with the red petals of General McArthur, Ena Harkness or Charles Mallerin, adding water and bringing to the boil. Allow to cool with the cover still on and pink rose-water for the hands and face will be ready when cool and strained.

CHAPTER XVIII

FRAGRANT TREES

"IN July", wrote Francis Bacon, in his essay *Of Gardens*, "come, musk roses, the lime-tree in blossom, early pears and plums in fruit." Is there a more summery perfume than that given off by the blossom of the lime tree so beloved by bees and from which they make that distinctly flavoured lime-green honey. Midday is the best time to enjoy the lime tree and in mid-July when the summer sun is at its hottest, and there beneath its shade one may lie listening to the roaring buzz of the bees and gradually become drowsy with the scent of the masses of greenish-white blossoms. The lime was planted during the eighteenth century in vast quantities, for its wood was soft and the one most easily carved by the artistic wood-workers of those days, those superb artists Grinling Gibbons and Samuel Watson of Chatsworth fame. The lime too was a tree which soon made its mark on the landscape and unfolding its pale green leaves early in summer it was much used by the landscape gardeners of the eighteenth century, Capability Brown and William Kent. Today it seems to have lost much of its popularity and so many of those eighteenth century limes have since been cut that the tree is in danger of becoming as rare as the once familiar, but now uncommon walnut. Plant it as abundantly as you may for it is a tree most suitable for the smaller garden and planted at 6 ft. apart will quickly hide an unsightly view. But more especially plant it for the delicious fragrance of its blossom in mid-summer.

One of the loveliest sights in my garden is the border planted against the prevailing winds of mixed standard trees, the limes, laburnums, flowering cherries and almonds, the May, all blending into the landscape as they flower in early summer. True, they are all in bloom at the same time and by mid-summer the display is over except for the various greens of their foliage, but what a tremendous show they make with the late flowering daffodils beneath. All these deliciously scented flowering trees are used in the standard form to which they are best suited and none is lovelier than the almond-scented Laburnum *L. Vossii*, with its extremely long golden racemes is the outstanding variety. Plant it near the limes or close to cupressus trees to enjoy the golden blooms to perfection.

Then the May, about which poets have shown their appreciation since earliest days. Is there a more delicious perfume than that of the May blossom of the hedgerow? It is the creamy white variety that carries the richest perfume, both the single and double varieties, but plant with them as a contrast the well-known Paul's Scarlet and Crataegus (which is the correct name for the thorn) Rosea, a double dusky pink variety which carries just a slight fragrance.

Here and there plant the Eucalyptus Poplar, *P. trichocarpa,* with its attractive narrow dark foliage, the best of the Balsam scented poplars and which does not make the rank growth that so many of them do. This is a tree which is delightfully scented after a summer shower and in early evening when dew is collecting about the foliage.

The tulip tree too, bears attractively sweet scented blooms. It may be likened to the magnolia in habit and also because its flowers do not appear until the tree is long established. Correctly called *Liriodendron tulipifera*, the small red and gold flowers of tulip shape possess a rich sweet perfume.

Several of the magnolias are difficult to establish and take several years to come into bloom, but if a choice is made carefully there are a number of quite easily grown varieties which will also bloom early. Probably the best known is *M. grandiflora*, which bears its rich lemon-scented creamy-white blooms early in summer, but which produces no bloom until at least twelve years old. But if the new Exmouth Variety of the same species is selected, with its broader leaves and larger blooms it will come into flower when about four years old.

June flowering and quite hardy is *M. Sinensis*, its pure white blooms being very sweetly scented and the same may be said of *M. Soulangiana*, which bears its blooms in April before its leaves. A hybrid from this species, *M. Lennei*, bears blooms of a rich rosy-purple colour and possessing a slight but pleasing perfume. Though each of these magnolias will grow well in a chalky soil, they will be happiest if planted with plenty of peat about their roots, and it is advisable to cover the roots with straw or bracken during winter.

Closely allied to the magnolias in soil requirements and habit are the rhododendrons, of which several species bear sweetly scented flowers. They may be classed as shrubs rather than trees but are generally planted in the woodland garden and so will not be out of place in this chapter. Few of the large flowered hybrid rhododendrons possess any perfume, but several of the species do so and all are intolerant of lime and so should be planted in beds of peat. One of the loveliest and most richly scented is *R. flavum luteum*, which makes a tall bush often 10-12 ft. in height. The pale yellow flowers, rather like those of the azalea are very richly scented. It is in fact, one of the parents of the Ghent azaleas, and so may be said to contain more azalea blood than of the rhododendron. Also strong growing is *R. Fortunei*, which bears masses of deliciously scented pale-pink flowers in early May. It is an extremely hardy species and bears long pointed, pale-green leaves which appear most attractive with the shell-pink blooms. Of the brilliantly flowered azaleas, *A. pontica*, known as the honey-suckle azalea, on account of its clusters of honey-scented amber coloured flowers, is a delightful plant, enhanced by its foliage turning rich crimson in autumn. Most of its hybrids possess the same sweet scent with their foliage taking on the crimson colourings in autumn. One of the loveliest is the double pale yellow *A. narcissiflora*, and the salmon-pink Bouquet de Flore. Heureuse Surprise, bears ivory-white flowers which are richly fragrant.

No shrubbery or woodland garden may be said to be complete without a few plants of the flowering currant, *Ribes sanguineum*, and its hybrids for not only do they provide a splash of rich colour during spring time, but the pale green foliage possesses a rich musky aroma, very much in fact like the blackcurrant. The richest coloured variety is *R. atrorubens* which produces its blood-red flowers in April.

The first flowering tree of spring is the almond, *Prunus*

amygdalus, the hybrid *Pollardii*, being a great improvement on the old common almond. It covers itself in its large deep pink flowers early in March and they carry a delicate almond fragrance. The tree will, in a good soil attain a height of 20 ft. and should be given plenty of room. The variety *rosea plena*, which bears attractive double rose flowers in profusion and which are also fragrant, is slower growing, rather later to come into bloom and is perhaps a better tree for a small garden than *Pollardii*. As with the flowering cherries, the almonds like a soil containing plenty of lime, as do all stone fruits; without it they make only limited growth as particularly does the species *dehiscens*. This is a little known but extremely hardy almond which bears masses of large single peach coloured blossoms during April and May and which carry a pleasing perfume.

Of the flowering cherries, *Prunus demissa*, a native of the U.S.A. makes a charming small tree bearing its fragrant white flowers in May and these give way to golden-yellow fruits in late summer.

The bird cherries, Cerasus or *Prunus padus* bear fragrant flowers, none more richly scented than the double white variety, *padus plena*. This is a strong growing tree, blooming in early summer. But none of the flowering cherries are as richly coloured nor as fragrant as *Cerasus Lannesiana*, the parent of many of the delightful hybrid cherries from Japan. One of its most interesting offspring is the variety, *Temari*, which bears both single and double flowers of a pale apple-blossom pink during April and which carry an apple-blossom fragrance. Extremely hardy and free flowering is the variety *affinis*, which covers itself with pure white cherry-like blossom early in May and which is richly almond scented. Most widely grown of the cherries in its native Japan is Yoshino, which makes a very large tree and is the first of all the Japanese cherries to come into flower. The blush-white blooms held in clusters possess a sweet fragrance.

A very handsome summer flowering tree is *Ptelea trifoliata*, known as the hop tree on account of its sweetly scented greenish-white flowers being likened to those of the hop, in their perfume. Though quite slow growing the tree will eventually reach a height of 18 ft. and is worth planting in every garden for its wood is also extremely aromatic.

A superb shrub-like tree for planting in a shaded corner and in a lime-free soil is the *Pieris*. In early summer the *Pieris Forrestii*, produces its rosettes of rhododendron-like leaves which are of vivid crimson, almost flower-like in their form. Later come the fragrant white flowers borne in long sprays. Similar in habit and colourings is *P. Formosa*, both being worthy of a corner sheltered from the cold spring winds.

Several of our most fragrant shrubs are suitable only in the mild climate of the south-west, one being the richly aromatic *Aloysia citridora*, the Lemon verbena, its foliage being so aromatic that a whole garden is scented in the gentle breeze of the south-west coast. But even there, a too rich soil will cause excessive growth which may be damaged during the winter. It needs, like the broom, a dry impoverished soil so that its wood can be hardened and making it not only better able to stand up to the cold winds but in addition bringing out to the full the rich lemon fragrance of its foliage. Mimosa too, which may be seen in all its Continental glory in nearly every garden of Falmouth, is far too tender for more exposed areas. Here it blooms in profusion during early spring and is cut and sent to Covent Garden for later use in our homes. There is no perfume quite like that of *Acacia dealbata*, the hardiest of the mimosas, its richness being almost intoxicating on a calm, warm day. Its foliage, which always looks so delicate, is ever-green which makes it so valuable a plant for the sheltered coastal districts of the south-west.

Richly fragrant are the blooms of *Choisya ternata*, commonly known as the Mexican Orange Flower, which seems to be quite hardy in southern gardens and even as far north as Gloucester, if given a warm, sheltered border and where it may receive some protection by taller growing trees. It will make a large bush, some 10 ft. tall, the glossy green leaves being evergreen with the clusters of milky-white flowers appearing in mid-summer. Where possible plant it near to a window where the rich perfume of the flowers may be enjoyed during the warm days of summer.

Requiring similar conditions does *Clerodendron trichotomum*, a Japanese shrub which is valuable in that it bears its fragrant white blooms in early September, being one of the few trees or shrubs to flower at this time of the year. Additional charm may be obtained from its vivid blue-black berries which are found after the flowers. Also producing masses of icy-white blooms in early autumn is *C. Fargessii*, of the same species and which is rather more shrub-like in its habit.

Not by any means a tree, but a shrub so valuable for covering a low wall in the springtime is the ornamental quince, the Cydonia, and my favourite of all shrubs. It would however, not have been mentioned in this book but for the appearance of *C. Maulei superba*, which bears the same glorious single cherry-scarlet blooms as does the more common *C. Japonica*, but with *Maulei*, they possess a distinct sweet fragrance, whilst later they give way to fruits like small golden-yellow apples. But its habit is more dwarf than the Japonica hybrids and it will have its own place in the garden, grown against a low wall or to the front of a shrub border.

To close on a most interesting and unusual shrub, *Colletia armata*, a native of Chile. Use it as a hedge for its wood is covered in strong needle-like thorns and though it produces but few leaves it covers itself with masses of snow-like flowers during October just when you are beginning to think that all is over for the season in the garden. The blossoms, like tiny white bells, appear almost overnight and carry a powerful honeysuckle fragrance. A most interesting plant.

INDEX

Abronia fragrans, 27
  latifolia, 27
Acacia dealbata, 154
Alecost, 106
Allwoodii, 70, 75
  alpinus, 77
  varieties, 75
Aloysia citriodora, 122, 154
Alyssum, sweet. *See* Annuals.
Androsace arachnoidea, 117
  chamaejasme, 117
  lanuginosa, 117
Annuals, use of, 47
  alyssum, sweet, 52
  calendula, 54
  candytuft (*Iberis odorata*), 54
  Dianthus Chinensis, 48
    Delight, 48
    Pink Bedder, 49
    Red Bedder, 49
  Limnanthes, 55
  marigold, French (*Tagetes signata*), 54
  mignonette, 17, 47, 51
  nasturtium, 53
    use of seed and leaves, 53
  stocks, 52, 17
  sweet peas, 47, 55
Anthemis nobilis. See Camomile.
Anthyllis montana, 113
Apple blossom, 17
  fragrant wood, 11, 12, 125, 135
  perfume of fruit, 11, 14
  varieties:
    Arthur Turner, 50, 129
    Brownlee's Russet, 129
    Cider Apples, 129
    Claygate Pearmain, 129
    Cornish Aromatic, 15
    D'Arcy Spice, 15, 18, 135
    Devonshire Quarrenden, 15, 135
    Egremont Russet, 135
    Orlean's Reinette, 135
    Pineapple Russet, 135
    St. Edmund's Russet, 135
Auricula, 32
  alpine, 38, 40
  garden, 39, 40
Azalea narcissiflora, 152
  pontica, 152

Bacon Francis, 13, 31, 54, 97, 102, 131, 150

Balm, 106
Bardswell, Frances, 65, 105, 106, 115
Bay, 17, 106, 122, 148
Berberis aquifolia, 124, 127
Bergamot (*Monarda*), 13, 22, 60, 64, 104
Biennials, cheiranthus, 50
  Oenothera biennis (evening primrose), 62
  Salvia harminum, 50
  stocks, East Lothian, 51
  sweet-william. *See* Dianthus.
  wallflower, 17, 49, 50, 91
Blackberry, 12, 131, 134
Blackcurrant, 133
Blind people, 16
Bluebell. *See* Scilla.
Bracken, fragrance of, 12, 32
  use of 22, 132
Buddleia, 16, 20, 71, 137
  culture, 138
  species:
    alternifolia, 139
    auriculata, 140
    globosa, 140
    variabilis, 139

Calamintha, 118
  suaveolens, 119
Camellia, oleifera, 124
  Sassanqua rubra, 124
  Williamsi Lanarth, 124
Camomile, 23, 112
Campion. *See* Lychnis.
Camphorosma Monspeliacum, 123
Candytuft. *See* Annuals.
Carnation, border, 72, 79
  culture, 80
  varieties, 81
Cerasus affinis, 153
  Lannesiana, 153
  Temari, 153
Chimonanthus fragrans, 21, 121
Choisya ternata, 154
Christmas roses. *See* Helleborus.
Chrysanthemum, 125
  Korean, 125
Cistus ladaniferus, 124
Clerodendron Fargessii, 155
  trichotomum, 154
Colletia armata, 155
Convallaria (lily-of-the-valley), 61
Crataegus (May), 151

Crocus longiflorus, 95
  vernus, 95
  versicolour, 95
Cyclamen Europaeum, 101
Cydonia alba, 123
  japonica, 123
  Maulei, 155

Damson, 129, 134
Daphne Blagayona, 118
  mezereum, 20, 117
  oneorum, 117
  rupestris, 118
  Somerset, 20
  striata, 118
Delphinium brunonianum, 22, 68
Dianthus, 69
  alpinus, 118
  as a rock plant, 76
  Blue, 79
  Boydii, 118
  caesius, 78
  caryophyllus, 69, 79
  Crossways, 78
  deltoides, 78, 118
  du Barry, 78
  Highland Queen, 78
  Little Jock, 78
  Loveliness, 79
  multiflorus, 78
  neglectus, 78
  Subacaulis, 78
  sweet-william, 47, 48
  Sweet Wivelsfield, 79
Dictamnus fraxinella, 64

Evening primrose, 24, 62

Featherfew, 104
Freesia, 101

Galanthus nivalis, 93
  plicatus, 93
Geranium, scented-leaf, 15, 17, 42, 82, 148
  culture, 83
  species:
    asperum, 86
    capitatum, 84, 86
    clorinda, 84
    crispum minor, 84
    crispum variegatum, 84
    filicifolium, 85
    fragrans, 85
    Graveolens, 84
    ibericum, 67
    marorhizum, 67
    nervosum, 85
    odoratissimum, 86
    Pretty Polly, 85
    Prince of Orange, 85
    Purple Unique, 86
    quercifolium, 85
    radula rosea, 86
    Rollinson's Unique, 86
    Scarlet Unique, 86
    stenopelatum, 86
  use in the home, 83
Gerard, 33, 96, 142
Gooseberry, 130
  fragrance of leaves, 131, 133
  varieties:
    Champagne Red, 131
    Glencarse Muscat, 130
    Gunner, 130
    Hebburn Prolific, 130
    Langley Beauty, 130
    Langley Gage, 130
    Pilot, 130
    Whitesmith, 131

Hamamelis arborea rubra, 121
  mollis, 20, 120
  vernalis, 121
  Virginiana, 20, 121
Heather, 12
Heliotrope, 30, 66
Helleborus altifolius, 126
  Bath Variety, 126
  niger, 126
  St. Brigid, 126
Herbaceous border, 59
Herbs, drying, 111
  use of, 104
Herrick, Robert, 147
Hesperis matronalis, 26
Honeysuckle, 12, 17, 19, 28, 55, 105, 120, 148. *See also* Lonicera.
Hyacinth, culture, 97
  Roman, 98
  varieties, 97
Hyssop, 23, 107

Incense, 15
Iris histrioides, 95
  Reticulata, 22, 94
  Stylosa, 95

Jasmine species:
  nudiflorum, 30
  officinale, 30
  stephanense, 30

Laburnum Vossii, 151
Laurus nobilis, 122
Lavender, 13, 17, 42, 60, 105, 107, 123, 148
  alba, 22, 108
  Cotton, 107
  Dutch, 108

Lavender (*contd.*)
  Folgate Blue, 108
  Grappenhall, 22, 108
  Hidcote, 22, 108
  Loddon Pink, 108
  Munstead, 108
  Old English, 108
  Seal, 108
Lawson, William, 69
Leaves, squeezing, 18
Leucojum aestivum, 100
Lilac, 14, 20
Lily, 17, 21
  species:
    cernuum, 22
    Hansoni, 100
    Henryi, 100
    pardalinum, 21
    pumilum, 22
    regale, 21, 100
    speciosum, 22
Lime, 135, 150
Linnarea borealis, 26
Liriodendron tulipifera, 151
Lonicera belgica, 29
  Caprifolium, 29
  fragrantissima, 120
  grata, 29
  Halleana, 29
  japonica aureo reticulata, 29
  periclymenum, 29
  purpusi, 121
  serotina, 29
Lupin, tree, 67
Lychnis vespertina, 26

Maeterlinck, Maurice, 18
Magnolia grandiflora, 151
  Lennei, 151
  Sinensis, 151
Marjoram, 108, 148
Matthiola bicornis. *See* Stocks.
McIntosh, 97
Micrimeria Corsica, 116
Mignonette. *See* Annuals.
Mimosa. *See* Acacia.
Mint, 13, 102, 109
  Apple, 109
  Bergamot-scented, 109
  black peppermint, 109
  catmint, 65, 70, 104
  corn, 109
  eau-de-Cologne, 23, 109
  Ginger, 109
  Japanese, 109
  Lemon, 109
Monarda. *See* Bergamot.
Muscari comosum, 94
  moschatum, 94
  Tubergenianum, 94

Narcissus Campernelles, 99
  Canalicatus, 99
  gracilis, 99
  jonquils, 94, 99
  recurvus, 100
  Tazetta, 99
  triandrus, 99
Nasturtium. *See* Annuals.
Nepeta (catmint), 65
  its culture, 66
Nicotiana affini, 25, 47
  sylvestris, 25

Oenothera missouriensis, 116
Onosma tauricum, 116
Osmarea Burkwoodii, 20

Pansy, 45
Parkinson, 15, 32, 33, 36, 38, 49, 54,
    68, 81, 96, 98, 103, 107, 112, 141
Parsley, 115
Paving, crazy, 19, 23, 26, 71, 109, 112,
  117
Pear, varieties:
  Conference, 130
  Jargonelle, 130
  Josephine de Malines, 130
  Pitmaston Duchess, 130
  Seckle, 130
Peat, burning, 12
  use of, 28, 34
Pelargonium. *See* Geranium.
Pennyroyal, 112, 115
Peony, 14, 59, 62
  its culture, 63
  Duchesse de Nemours, 22
  Sarah Bernhardt, 63
Pests, Red Spider, 44
Philadelphus (mock orange), 14, 20
  coronarius, 20
Pieris Formosa, 154
  Forrestii, 20, 154
Pinks, 21, 68, 70
  culture, 72
  varieties:
    Bridal Veil, 73
    Dusky, 73, 148
    Glory of Lyonaise, 21, 73
    Her Majesty, 73
    Ice Queen, 73
    Jane Austen, 21, 73
    Laced, 74, 75
    Ludford Pink, 73
    Mrs. Sinkins, 73
    Old Cottage Pink, 74
    Red Emperor, 21
    Sam Barlow, 74
    Show, 76
    Sutton Pink, 74
    Victorian, 21, 75
    White Ladies, 74

Plum, 134
  varieties:
    Laxton's Delight, 134
    Oullin's Golden Gage, 134
    Severn Cross, 134
Polyanthus, Barrowby Gem, 100, 126
Poplar trichocarpa, 151
Pot-pourii, 82, 104
Primrose, 12, 17, 32
  double, 33
  hose-in-hose, 36
  Jack-in-the-Green, 36
  Juliae Craddock's White, 38, 127
    Garryardes, 37
    hybrids, 37
    Wanda, 37
  sowing the seed, 38
  varieties:
    alba plena, 33, 35
    Bon Accord Blue, 36
    Bon Accord Elegans, 35
    Bon Accord Gem, 35
    Bon Accord Purity, 36
    Chevithorne Pink, 36
    Crathes Crimson, 36
    Green, 17
    Marie Crousse, 28, 35, 91, 100
    Quaker's Bonnet, 35
    Red Paddy, 35
    Sulphur, 32
Primula, Asiatic, 27
  culture of, 27
  species:
    florindae, 28
    helodoxa, 28
    nutans, 28
    pubescens, 40
    Sikkimensis, 27
Prunus amygadalus, 153
  dehiscens, 153
  demissa, 153
  padus, 153
  rosea plena, 153
Ptelea trifoliata, 153

Raspberry, 17, 132
  autumn-fruiting, 133
Rea, John, 33
Rhododendron flavum luteum, 152
  Fortunei, 152
Ribes atrorubens, 152
  sanguineum, 152
Robinson, William, 26, 38, 61, 62, 67, 116, 122
Rohde, Eleanour Sinclair, 15, 52, 97
Rosemary, 13, 17, 23, 60, 104, 105, 110, 120, 123, 148
Roses, dried petals, 14, 105, 148
  species:
    Austrian briar, 143
    Bourbon, 144

Cabbage, 141
China, 144
Damask, 143
Floribunda, 146
Gallica, 142
Hybrid teas, 145
  Caroline Testout, 145
  Charles Mallerin, 145, 148
  Crimson Glory, 147
  Ena Harkness, 19, 53, 146
  Etoile de Hollande, 146
  Forty-Niner, 145
  General McArthur, 145
  Gloire de Dijon, 147
  Golden Dawn, 146
  Marcelle Gret, 146
  McGredy's Ivory, 146
  Sutter's Gold, 146
  Tahiti, 14, 35, 145, 148
  The Doctor, 146
  Verschuren's Pink, 146
Moss, 143
Musk, 147
Provence roses, 141
Rue, 104

Sage, 23, 60, 102, 110
Salvia argenta, 67
  azurea, 67
  nemorosa, 22
  patens, 68
Santolina, 107
Scilla alba, 96
  amethystina, 96
  italica, 96
  nutans, 96
  pratensis, 96
Shakespeare, 29, 112, 143, 147
Sleep, procuring, 14, 42, 50, 87
Snowdrop. *See* Galanthus.
Solomon's seal, 61, 104
Southernwood, 13, 16, 85, 105, 111, 148
Stocks, night-scented, 24, 47
Strawberries, fragrance of foliage, 13, 17, 131
  fragrance of fruit, 13, 130
  fragrant varieties, 132
  perpetual-fruiting, 132
Sweet Peas. *See* Annuals.
Sweet Rocket. *See Hesperis.*

Tagetes signata. See Annuals.
Tarragon, 111
Thyme, 13, 113, 148
  species:
    argenta, 114
    aureus, 114
    carnosus, 114
    coccineus, 113
    Corsicus, 114

Thyme, species (*contd.*)
  fragrantissimus, 114
  herba barona, 114
  lanuginosus, 113
  lemon-scented, 23, 105, 113, 148
  minimus, 114
  serpyllum, 113
Tobacco plant. *See Nicotiana.*
Tubs, planting of, 86, 106
Tulips for bedding, 50, 89
  for perfume, 88
  for pot culture, 88
  species:
    australis, 91
    persica, 91
    sylvestris, 91
  varieties:
    Cherbourg, 90
    Cordelia, 90
    Crown Imperial, 88
    Demeter, 90
    Fred Moore, 88
    Golden Age, 91
    Marietta, 90
    Marquette, 89
    Mrs. Moon, 90
    Murillo, 89
    Nauticus, 90
    Philippe de Commines, 90

Primrose Beauty, 90
Prince of Austria, 88
Schoonoord, 89
Tearose, 89
White Victory, 91
Yellow Prince, 88

Verbena canadensis, 66
  corymbosa, 22, 66, 148
  tridens, 66
Viburnum carlesii, 19
  fragrans, 19
  henryi, 19
Viola, 45, 60
  winter-flowering, 127
Violet, 12, 17, 32, 42, 131
  varieties:
    Admiral Avellan, 44
    Coeur d'Alsace, 44
    Comte de Brazza, 44
    Czar, 44
    Marie Louise, 44
Violettas, 46

Window-box, 32, 37, 46, 77, 85, 115, 126
Wine, plants for flavouring, 69
Witch-hazel. *See Hamamelis.*